# CARTER BROWN

# READY WHEN YOU ARE, C.B.!

## THE AUTOBIOGRAPHY OF ALAN YATES
### ALIAS CARTER BROWN

## ABOUT *UNTAPPED*

Most Australian books ever written have fallen out of print and become unavailable for purchase or loan from libraries. This includes important local and national histories, biographies and memoirs, beloved children's titles, and even winners of glittering literary prizes such as the Miles Franklin Literary Award.

Supported by funding from state and territory libraries, philanthropists and the Australian Research Council, *Untapped* is identifying Australia's culturally important lost books, digitising them, and promoting them to new generations of readers. As well as providing access to lost books and a new source of revenue for their writers, the *Untapped* collaboration is supporting new research into the economic value of authors' reversion rights and book promotion by libraries, and the relationship between library lending and digital book sales. The results will feed into public policy discussions about how we can better support Australian authors, readers and culture.

See untapped.org.au for more information, including a full list of project partners and rediscovered books.

*Readers are reminded that these books are products of their time. Some may contain language or reflect views that might now be found offensive or inappropriate.*

# CONTENTS

# PUBLISHER'S NOTE

Of all the characters Alan Yates, or Carter Brown, has created, none is more popular nor unorthodox than Al Wheeler, that undeniable Lieutenant from the Pine City Sheriff's Office.

Lieutenant Wheeler has never been one to keep his sleuth's nose out of things—and this autobiography of his creator is no exception. He certainly denies not being 'real'.

That is why you will find his interjections throughout the text. They are set in italics and followed by the initials 'A.W.' for Al Wheeler.

Not to be outdone, the author replies angrily to these Wheeler interjections with his own initials 'A.Y.' for Alan Yates.

When they made their pitch to him about writing his autobiography I didn't say a word. I've been a cop long enough to know when to keep my mouth shut. But, right off, I could see it making a big fun book stretching to around five pages of easy-to-read print and maybe it would include a real cute picture of him surrounded by his glasses. Well, like his father said, we all make mistakes. I figured I would just hang around, preferably with a couple of well-stacked blondes for company, and wait until his sanity returned. Then he could get back to reality, recording the cases and the women in the life and times of Lieutenant Al Wheeler.

The unorthodox cop.

From the sheriff's office.

Me.

But after a while I started getting this uneasy feeling in the pit of my stomach. After all, we've been together in a real close association over the last twenty years and it's not my fault I stay an immutable thirty-five while he keeps on getting older every year.

Some have got it, some haven't.

Still, and all, I didn't want to see him make another pratfall. Ever since he was a small kid he's been bouncing along life's merry highway on his ass. I figured the least I could do was to help him out. Okay, so I don't have any credits as a writer. Frankly, I have better ways to spend my evenings, like chasing the luscious honey-blonde Annabelle Jackson around my oversized couch, but I know how it's done. No, not that. I'm talking about writing. I've looked over his hunched shoulders long enough to pick it up. You grab hold of a bunch of words and put them into some kind of order. Well, that's the way he does it. Only it's not enough for an autobiography.

Selective highlights is the keynote. Who the hell wants to know

*you spent all day staring hopelessly at the blank page in the type-
writer then, come nightfall, you kicked the cat and went to bed. Or
the real exciting time when the doctor said he didn't figure you were
pregnant, more like it was a gall bladder attack. And the hell with
chronological order. You start off saying. 'It was raining the day I
was born', and the first thing you know your reader has switched on
the television and thrown your book out of the window. On the first
page you've got to grab your reader by the short hairs and pull them
straight into the book. Like I've just done to you, right? (You'll have to
speak up, I don't hear negatives too good.)*

*The reason I know these things is because I'm just that much
smarter than he is. It's no great trick to be that way. Most of us are.
So I've written up some of the highlights. He needs all the help he can
get. And they are all written at a fast pace with no intellectual crap
and are exciting, fascinating, and unputdownable. Confidentially, if
you just skip the in-between bits it won't be any big loss.*

(For the last ten years, Lieutenant Al Wheeler has been hoping to make Captain. Fat Chance! A.Y.)

# CHAPTER ONE
# A LIFE ON THE OCEAN WAVE

'You are appointed to HMS *Golden Hind*, Sydney, Australia, for onward disposal', said the formal letter from the Admiralty.

HMS *Golden Hind*. The name sang. It was pure poetry, evocative of the Spanish Main and derring-do. I found out later that its only claim to fame was its mosquitoes which were compared to Stuka dive-bombers. And as well as being known as HMS *Golden Hind*, it was also known in its less fancy moments as Warwick Farm Racecourse. But ignorance was still bliss as I re-read the letter. I already had a great deal of affection for Australians because one of them, Lionel Van Praag, had captained West Ham's speedway team when I was a devoted twelve-year-old supporter and, at the age of fifteen, I had seen Stan McCabe make a magnificent knock of eighty-one against Middlesex in something like forty-one minutes. Even if Sydney was some 10 000 miles away from England, I did know something about it. You would find kangaroos bounding along their main streets and they also had a wonderful beach called Bondi Beach. That was the way it was spelled but it was pronounced, 'Bondee'. Everybody knew that.

I had joined the Royal Navy in September 1942 and became a member of the crew of a Landing Craft Infantry (Small) some six months later. They were the elite of landing craft, designed as Commando raiding craft, and not dissimilar to motor torpedo boats in appearance. I stayed with her through the invasion of Europe then in October 1944 some eager beaver in Admiralty discovered the letter recommending me for a commission that my skipper had sent some fifteen months before. So when I received the magic letter in January 1945, I had risen from the

rank of Able Seaman to the heady heights of an acting temporary Sub-lieutenant of the Royal Naval Volunteer Reserve.

The voyage to Australia in a troopship took nineteen days
with the ship making one stop of six hours' duration at Colon,
on the mouth of the Panama Canal, but nobody was allowed
ashore. The only things of interest I remember seeing were my
first flying fish and the Southern Cross. The ship arrived in Sydney around seven in the morning and I stood on deck with my
mouth wide open just not believing it as vista after vista of the
harbour unrolled in front of my enchanted eyes.

After we docked, the bad news was that HMS *Golden Hind*
was full, so I and another junior officer would have to stay in a
private hotel on Bondi Beach—with an extra living allowance
provided, of course.

It looked like things were tough all over.

My last memory of the troopship was seeing the disconso-
late-looking group of Wrens standing huddled together close
to the gangway. During the voyage they had turned up their
noses at us British lads and fallen for the sophisticated blan-
dishments of the returning Australian airmen who all seemed
to have at least one DFC to go with their wings. But now all the
Australian flyers were busy on the dockside being reunited
with their wives, sweethearts, and any etcetera they felt in need
of. And it served the Wrens right, we losers generously thought
as we walked down the gangway to set foot on Australian soil
for the first time.

We had lunch at the Tarleton Hotel then went for a walk in
the afternoon and, oh, my God!, there was a shop actually selling fruit. We bought enough to make ourselves sick a couple of
hours later, then discovered a milk bar further down the street.
The whole street was probably a mirage but we determined to
make the most of it while it lasted. The girl who served us asked
if we were from London. My friend was a Scot and while he was
still sneering I told the girl I was a Londoner.

'Gee!' She looked suitably impressed, 'Were you there in the

Blitz?' I said I was and modestly prepared to tell her about the night the East End was hit and the Thames was at its lowest ebb and ... but I was wasting my time.

'I bet it was almost as bad as it was here', the girl interrupted me. 'You must have heard about the Japanese submarine that got into our harbour. It was terrible!'

Night came and brought no blackout with it. Australia was obviously a fantasy land and I intended to make the most of it. And I did for the next six days until the Navy caught up with me again. There was a wonderful lost weekend in the middle. Somehow I met a bunch of American marines who were all fighter pilots. They were finishing a two weeks' leave and invited me to their farewell party on the Friday night. I arrived at the house they were renting around eight that night and left sometime around eight the following Monday morning. When I try and remember the weekend in detail it seems to be almost totally obscured in an alcoholic fog. But I do remember drinking with a Captain in the kitchen late on the Saturday evening when an immaculately-dressed Major appeared with a very attractive blonde on his arm.

'Major', the Captain said politely. 'This limey is Alan Yates.'

'Hi', the Major said, then looked at the blonde. 'Say hello to the Lootenant, honey.'

'Hello', the blonde said dutifully.

'Okay', the Major said briskly, 'that's enough socialising. Now let's get down to the fornicating'.

It wasn't so much that the Americans had style, I thought wistfully, as I watched them disappear into the nearest vacant bedroom, but far more importantly they had girls, too.

Our only duty was to ring the Captain's secretary (a prematurely-balding Lieutenant) once a day to find out if he had any news for us. On the seventh day, he did. We had been appointed to the Fourth Cruiser Squadron for still more onward disposal and we were to be on board a destroyer, HMS *Quilliam*, by five that afternoon. The British Pacific Fleet was in Leyte.

*Quilliam* was joining it and so were we.

Being a passenger in a naval ship is really boring. All day to do and nothing to do, except try and stay out of other people's way. The only thing that broke the monotony was when *Quilliam* hit the centre of a typhoon and had to heave-to for twelve hours. The Captain used his sea cabin on the bridge while the ship was at sea so I, as a passenger, had the use of his day cabin. The bed was so narrow that I spent a wonderful night while the ship was hoved-to, lying on the bed with both arms fully outstretched and my hands desperately clutching the sides of the bed as it tilted from side to side at impossible angles. Sleep was completely impossible so I had plenty of time to reflect on some of the more memorable times I had spent during the two previous years in landing craft.

*(It's real pathetic. Only a few goddamned pages into the book and he's starting to twitch already. What kind of a transition is that? If it was a movie, they'd have to have a sub-title that said* FLASHBACK *in big letters and went on and off like a neon sign the whole time. A.W.)*

After four months of basic training I was sent to Troon, the Combined Operations base on the west coast of Scotland for further training and to be ultimately drafted to a landing craft. One Friday afternoon I was given a draft-chit to LCI(S) 504 and a single ticket to Glasgow. So off I went, complete with kitbag, hammock and suitcase, and arrived in Glasgow around five in the afternoon. It was early 1943 and Combined Operations was still regarded with deep suspicion by the regular naval personnel, especially the Chief Petty Officer at the naval transport office, who had been called out of retirement at the beginning of the war.

'Combined Operations', he said, and sniffed loudly. 'That's that little Sub-lieutenant with an office on the other side of the street. But there's no use you trying to see him now because he always pisses off real sharpish around three on a Friday afternoon.'

So he finally decided I should spend the weekend at a leave centre, and gave me a chit to make it possible, and also stern instructions to report to the little Sub-lieutenant in the Combined Operations office on the following Monday morning.

Halfway up one of the side streets leading away from the station, I realised I had forgotten to ask the whereabouts of Sauchiehall Street where the leave centre was situated. Fortunately for me help was close at hand. Leaning against the wall on the opposite side of the street was a lady wearing a tightly-belted raincoat, a jaunty beret, and smoking a cigarette. As she was obviously either taking a rest or waiting for somebody, I thought she was the ideal person to give me directions. So I crossed the street still carrying kitbag, hammock and suitcase, gave her a sunny smile and said, in my best English accent, 'Excuse me, Madame, but can you tell me the way to Sauchiehall Street?'

'Fuck off, you stupid Sassenach bastard', she said, with great contempt, and flicked ash all over the shiny toecaps of my naval issue boots.

The daily issue of the rum ration was an important event in our lives. Especially because in landing craft, as other small ships, it was issued neat. With a crew of fourteen entitled to draw their tot of rum, the coxswain would look the other way while you carefully bottled your tot for future use. The rum itself was something like 125 proof. You couldn't pour it into a glass because it was too thick and would only trickle.

When someone had a birthday they would be offered 'sippers' all round by the rest of the crew. On the lower deck dinner was at twelve noon and the rum was issued just before. So the happy birthday boy, having consumed some thirteen 'sippers' as well as his own tot would sit down to dinner at the messdeck table but rarely finish it. He would start a singsong all by himself, or loudly announce his intention of going up on deck to murder the skipper or, one time I especially remember, push the contents of his dinner plate into his neighbour's face because his neighbour hadn't passed the salt quickly enough. I happened to be his neighbour at the time. Whatever the reaction, the birthday boy would pass out cold and be laid to rest on the nearest seat. Around six in the evening you would hear loud groans and piteous whimperings about the state of his head, then he would sit up, the fumes would rise to his head, and he would be a cheap drunk for another fifteen minutes.

On board 504 were two close friends. Jock Allard was the dour, canny Glaswegian while Ginger McFee was the redheaded cyclone from Edinburgh. One summer evening, when we were moored in the middle of the Hamble River, Ginger decided he would have a run ashore. Jock decided he would remain on board. A passionate argument developed with Ginger McFee resorting to large swigs from his bottle of illegally-hoarded rum whenever he ran out of persuasive talk. Finally a compromise was reached. Ginger would have his run ashore and Jock would generously row him to the wharf in the craft's dinghy as it was now far too late to catch the official liberty boat.

So Jock rowed the dinghy around to the rope ladder that hung down one side of the craft and waited. Ginger emerged briskly from the messdeck hatchway, ran across the deck and descended the rope ladder even more briskly. The heel of his boot hit the bow of the dinghy and pushed it away. Undaunted, Ginger continued his rapid descent and disappeared into the river. He surfaced a few seconds later, his cap still firmly fixed on his head, and climbed the rope ladder back up onto the deck. From the moment he had first appeared from the messdeck hatchway, the whole scene had been conducted at silent film speed. Now, with water forming a large puddle around his feet, Ginger leaned over the guardrail and courteously thanked the bemused Jock for having brought him back from his run ashore. Then he returned to the messdeck, slung his hammock, stripped off his wet clothes, and was fast asleep five minutes later. From the next morning on, nobody could ever convince him that he hadn't spent the evening ashore drinking at the local pub.

There was an art to drinking naval rum neat. You had to ease it down your tongue then swallow slowly and carefully. If you allowed the rum to hit the back of your throat you would cough and choke helplessly until the fumes subsided. Of course, if you were already drunk you wouldn't care. To prove it, there were three deaths from asphyxiation in the LCI(S) flotilla over a period of eighteen months.

Came the invasion of Europe and 504 carried about a hundred of Lord Lovat's No. 1 Commando Brigade, landing them on the beach at Ouistreham. The Channel crossing was very rough and just about everybody on board was seasick. Afterwards, the only thing we could do was hose down the messdecks which meant everything ran down into the bilges and stayed there for the next month until the craft could be dry-docked and the bilges emptied and cleaned. But during that month the smell from the bilges permeated the whole craft below decks. The cook never cooked a hot meal during that period. We existed on cans of self-heating soup, cold provisions, and bars of chocolate. And everything eaten on the upper deck.

In later years when one of our children when very young was sick, my wife quickly got used to seeing me bravely rushing off in the opposite direction with one hand clapped over my mouth and my eyes rolling wildly. It was called an automatic reflex I would say weakly, and sometime later.

We were to land our commandos at H-Hour plus five minutes as the second wave to hit the beach. The first wave was a flotilla of Landing Craft Tank (Assault) whose job was to literally fling themselves onto the beach and disgorge their tanks onto it. A pall of dense mist hid the beach from us as we approached but we could hear the sound of gunfire and see the spurts of water around us as shells landed in the sea. Then, out of the mist came an LCT(A) with the whole of its well-deck on fire and obviously out of control. It seemed one hell of an introduction at the time.

When we did hit the beach, two ramps were pushed forward

over our bows by two seamen to each ramp until they dropped
onto the sand. Then the commandos ran down the ramps onto
the beach and immediately began their intricate pattern of
ever-changing formations as they advanced across the beach.
Meantime, one of our gunners who was a 'natural' was firing
tracer shells from his oerlikon gun into what had probably once
been a boarding house on the sea shore. Our gunner was out-
lining each window with his tracer and the windows seemed
to be disgorging an inordinate number of bodies. There was
still a hell of a lot of enemy fire hitting the beach, too. I looked
back over my shoulder at one moment and saw a big LCI approaching the beach astern of us and then a shell wiped out
her bridge completely. But then, thankfully, we had landed all
our commandos, could pull in our ramps and get the hell out of
there. Only their CO, who was a Major, complete with a genuine monocle, remembered his manners. While everybody else
was flattened to the deck, he stood in a couple of feet of water at
the bottom of one ramp, oblivious to what was going on around
him and gently waved his swagger-cane.

'Thanks awfully for the ride', he bawled at our skipper.
'Good show, that. Enjoyed every minute.'

Then he turned and walked slowly up the beach. Everyone
spontaneously recognised his bravery but it was Jock Allard who
put our feelings into words while the Major was still talking.

'Why doesn't somebody kill the stupid bastard,' Jock moaned,
'so we can fuck off out of here?'

About two weeks later we were doing a routine anti-midget
submarine patrol and saw three British minesweepers off Le
Havre, which was still held by the Germans. A few minutes
later a squadron of rocket-firing RAF Typhoons appeared out
of a cloudless blue sky. Within the next five minutes two of
the minesweepers were sunk, and the third was sinking. We
heard later that Naval Intelligence blamed RAF Intelligence for
not having warned the Typhoon squadron the minesweepers
would be in the area. RAF Intelligence counterclaimed they had

not been informed about the minesweepers at all. But by that time the argument would have become strictly academic.

We picked up a dozen survivors from the nearest sunken minesweeper and took them back to the artificial harbour that had been created at Arromanches. As we landed them, a pinkfaced midshipman, who was probably all of eighteen years of age, raced down the wharf to meet the men as they stepped ashore—all of them covered from head to foot with filthy black oil.

'I say', the midshipman panted breathlessly, 'are you men survivors?'

'No, mate', a burly stoker growled, 'we're bloody tourists!'

504 had been the first LCI(S) ever built and spent the first few months of her life based in Bo'ness, a tiny fishing port a good way up the Firth of Forth. We would take out training crews twice a week, down the Forth to the mouth, a quick venture into the North Sea, then spend the night at Methyl, which was a mining port, and return to Bo'ness the following day. It was a pleasant and uneventful existence while it lasted. I became good friends with the Petty Officer Motor Mechanic who was inevitably known as 'Mac'. He was about twenty-five and, from my nineteen-year-old outlook, was almost middle-aged. Before joining the Navy he had been a police driver with the Flying Squad.

One Sunday afternoon when we were enjoying a cup of tea in a canteen run by the local ladies of Bo'ness, one of them asked how we felt about going into action. Mac surprised me by saying he wasn't frightened by the thought of being killed. What really scared him was the thought of being maimed.

'If I was badly injured I wouldn't hang around to find out just how crippled I was going to be for the rest of my life', he said. 'I'd roll myself over the side and finish it.'

The Bo'ness lady was suitably impressed while I thought I had never heard such a load of bull in all my life.

A couple of months later we joined the rest of the flotilla

outside Southampton, then Mac was transferred to LCI(S) 509 shortly afterwards. D-Day and the invasion of Europe came and went. 504 returned to its base on the Hamble River sometime in mid-September and we all had leave. When I returned from the leave I found I was to report to Chatham barracks in two weeks' time for an officer's selection board. But, in the meantime, along came Operation Infatuate—something that 504 had absolutely nothing to do with, I'm grateful to say. Only four LCIs were involved, one of them acting as a temporary hospital ship.

In October 1944, the Canadians had taken the Belgian port of Antwerp but the Germans still barred the entrance to it. The only approach to Antwerp was along the River Scheldt, past the fortified island of Walcheren. Three LCI(S)s were to land Royal Marine Commandos at Westkapelle on the island. The Support Squadron Eastern Flank, consisting of twenty-five craft, firing guns, anti-aircraft guns, mortars, and rockets, would escort in the LCI(S)s to make their landings. In the event, Walcheren was one of the bloodiest naval actions of the war, and certainly the bloodiest where landing craft were concerned. Of the twenty-five craft belonging to the SSEF, nine were lost and nine others put out of action; 172 officers and men of their crews were killed and over 200 wounded. LCI(S) 532 was hit and blew up after having beached her Royal Marine Commandos.

One late October afternoon on the peaceful Hamble River, 509 came alongside us looking very battered indeed. I saw Shorty on deck, an ex-fisherman from Cornwall who I knew well. 'How was Walcheren?', I asked, and he told me in graphic detail.

'How's Mac?', I also asked when he had finished.

'He was halfway out of the engine room hatch as we were going into the beach, watching, like he always did', Shorty said. 'A shell exploded close to him and he was filled up with shrapnel. There was nothing we could do for him right then so we wrapped him in a blanket and lay him down on the deck near the stern. After we'd got off the beach we went back for him but he'd gone.'

'Gone?', I echoed.

'Must have thrown himself over the side', Shorty said indifferently. 'You remember Mac. He was always saying he'd do that if he got badly injured.'

And one final memory of my friend, Leo Clark. There were a half dozen of us who had been close at school and stayed in touch afterwards. Leo, aged seventeen, had advanced his age by two years and joined the RAF. He had learned to fly in Canada, and then had spent six months flying with the American Coastal Command before returning to England. We met him in the local pub. The rest of us were about to join the Army, the Navy, or the Air Force. And here was Leo Clark, resplendent in his sergeant-pilot's uniform, complete with the coveted wings on his chest. And the stories he told of America. How he'd met Betty Grable in Miami and how she had sunbaked topless on the beach. A topless Bette Grable? Our faces blanched and our knees weakened at the thought.

'Leo', one of us said hoarsely. 'You didn't. I mean, well, did you?'

'Don't be stupid', Leo said coldly. 'Betty Grable isn't only a big film star; she's also a lady. She was just being nice to some guys in uniform.'

It was a great night. I drank nine pints of beer, got home after midnight and was promptly sick all over the hall carpet. An action which did not delight my mother.

Two weeks later, at night, in the middle of a thick fog, Leo Clark flew his Blenheim bomber into the side of a mountain in northern Scotland.

·

*It was the kind of operation designed to sort out the men from the boys. The time was November 1943, and the place the English Channel. We carried No. 4 Commando with the objective of landing them* on the French coast near the mouth of the Somme. They figured on spending a couple of hours ashore, knocking over a German strong-point and maybe picking up a few prisoners. After we'd landed them, we were going to stooge around for a couple of hours then go back onto the beach and pick them up. Good old 504 was right up there in the front, like always.

The first night was a wipe-out. We were leaving a wake, bubbling with phosphorescence, a couple of miles astern. So we had to turn back. The second night, everything seemed just fine until we came with sight of the beach. They were having some kind of anti-invasion practice with searchlights turned on and shore batteries firing at a towed target ship. Almost immediately 504 executed a 180° turn. I didn't believe it. I didn't even want to believe it but I had to make sure. So I went up onto the bridge. There he was in silhouette against the floodlit sky in back of us, with the smaller figure of the First Lieu-tenant right there beside him.

'Capt'n', I said softly. 'Just what the hell is going on around here, exactly?'

He turned around to face me, his shoulders hunched, and there was a faint flash of reflected light from his wrap-around glasses.

'I can't do it, Al', he said tensely. 'It would be murder. Worse, even. Like suicide.'

In all my life so far he was the only guy I had ever allowed to call me Al, I remembered. It didn't make doing what I had to do any easier.

'This is the last night of no moon, Capt'n', I reminded him. 'No more chances after tonight.'

'It's too bad, Al', he said. 'I know just how you feel. Real frustrated and dejected. Believe me, I feel exactly the same. Worse, maybe.'

'You're lying, Capt'n', I said wearily. 'You're scared. You're more yellow than a banana in one of Carmen Miranda's hats!'

'Don't make it any tougher for me than it already is, Al', he pleaded.

Looking over his hunched shoulders at the writing on the fast-re-ceding beach, spelled out with searchlights, I realised I didn't have any choice. But, in fairness, I figured I should give him one last chance.

'Capt'n', I said softly. 'Below decks we've got over a hundred commandos, and all of them eating their hearts out to land on that beach and attack that strongpoint. They don't give a goddamn if they live or die, all they want is to get into action.'

'Maybe they don't care if they live or die', he said, with a slight sob in his voice, 'but I do, Al. I've got a lot of living to do yet. I want to go to Australia and eat fruit and get drunk and meet some girls, and things like that. Okay, if you want to call me a coward, call me a coward. So I'm a coward. But is wanting to live so you can keep on enjoying life all that wrong, Al? I mean, is it that bad, Al, that you have to ...'

He stopped talking right then because he'd run out of breath the moment after my stiffened fingers sank into his flabby solar plexus. As he started to double up I gave him a rabbit chop across the nape of his neck and he fell unconscious on the deck at my feet. It was the philosophy I just couldn't take any longer.

'Al!' the First Lieutenant said, in a shocked voice. 'This is mutiny!'

He was only a kid. A Midshipman and only eighteen years old. So I was only nineteen, but that year made a hell of a lot of difference. Like my voice had broken, and everything.

'You got to make a choice, kid', I told him. 'Either we turn this old tin can around and head straight back to that beach, or you're going to have to arrest me for mutiny. Or try, anyway. I don't fancy your chances because I'm betting I'll have a hundred commandos on my side. But the choice is all yours.'

I could hear him biting savagely on his lower lip. He was some kind of a masochist, too, and that didn't help a lot. But the next moment the agonising decision was taken out of his hands.

'Able Seaman', a deep voice said, from in back of me. 'I salute you!'

I turned around and saw the commando Major standing there. The myopic one with a monocle stuck in one eye.

'Well, thanks, Major', I shrugged modestly. 'It was nothing.'

'You're damned right', he said, 'and still is nothing while we're heading in the opposite direction to the beach'.

'One-eighty degrees to starboard', I yelled at the Coxswain.

'Starboard, one-eighty', he acknowledged.

504 turned in a graceful arc until she was heading back toward the beach again. Directly ahead of us shells from the shore battery made a direct hit on the German target vessel and it disappeared in a sheet of flame.

'That could be us five minutes from now', the First Lieutenant said nervously.

'What the hell, kid!' I grinned as I punched him lightly on the arm. 'You want to live forever?'

(The aborted operation did happen and certainly none of 504's crew were unhappy about never making the landing. One thing I can't understand in Wheeler's weird wonderland is how he ever came to invent a creep like the supposed captain. Hunched shoulders, wrap-around glasses, and some crazy desire to go to Australia and eat fruit? Wow! A.Y.)

# CHAPTER TWO
## LOVE AND MARRIAGE

Onward disposal finally came to an end when we reached Leyte and I joined HMS *Euryalus*. She was a light cruiser, improved *Dido* class, and could do around thirty-four knots flat out. She had a complement of approximately thirty-five officers and 600 men. I still have a picture somewhere of the whole ship's company but I've never actually counted them so I could be wrong. Being the only cypher officer on board I had my very own tiny cypher office and most of the time could dictate the hours I worked. It was always unfortunate that I was gallantly coping with a spate of secret signals whenever a senior officer wanted me to do something different.

In the five months that remained of the Pacific War, the British Pacific Fleet sailed the equivalent of three and a half times around the world and once spent fifty-two days at sea, returning to Manus Island, the big American base in the Admiralty Islands. About the only things available on Manus were long walks and warm beer. No Waves or nurses. We went for over three months without seeing a woman. Everybody knew what they were going to do when they first saw a woman again. They were going to grab hold of her, rip off all her clothes, then rape her twenty-five times in succession. Of course what actually happened when you finally did see your first woman was you gave her a polite smile and, if you were feeling particularly reckless, ventured a 'Good morning', or whatever, depending on the time of day. Reality was the death knell of phallic fantasies. Logic says there must have been some homosexual relationships on board every ship but I was never aware of them. Too naive, probably.

*(Or too fagged out? A.W.)*

There is the classic story, sworn to be true, of the cruiser captain in the North Sea sometime in early 1940 who cleared lower deck and, when his crew of 800 men were assembled on the quarterdeck, addressed them as follows. 'Men', he said solemnly, 'it's been brought to my attention that there is too much buggery going on in this ship. If it doesn't slacken off, I shall have to put a stop to it altogether'.

The BPF bombarded Sakishima Gunto, a group of islands I was convinced had previously been totally unknown and, immediately after the bombardment was finished, lapsed straight back into total obscurity again. At the same time the American Fleet was busy helping retake Okinawa and they didn't want us tagging along with them. The American Navy, with some justification, regarded the war in the Pacific as their war and they didn't want the British to intrude on any of their glory right at the end.

But there were compensations.

On our way to Sydney for twelve glorious days of leave, a pay Sub-lieutenant told me I must meet his girlfriend. She was not only a looker, he said, she was also a really nice girl. The last time he had seen her, her mother had been ill and his girlfriend had looked after her with some self-sacrifice and great competence. I was still suffering from post-Manus Island frenzy and asked if she had any nympho girlfriends she might introduce me to, which didn't go down too well. A couple of nights after the ship had arrived in Sydney, my friend invited his girlfriend and her mother on board to dinner and asked me if I would join them. That obviously translated as 'Would I look after the mother?' As it so happened I had nothing better to do. I was very impressed with the girlfriend and I even liked her mother. During the rest of our stay in Sydney I managed to see a lot more of my friend's girlfriend who, I discovered, didn't see herself as his girlfriend at all. Her name was Denise MacKellar.

She lived with her mother in Cremorne and Grace was separated from her father, Keith.

We spent the last five or six weeks of the war steaming up and down off the coast of Japan while the aircraft carriers flew off their planes to bomb Tokyo. About the only opposition we had was the kamikaze variety. I remember seeing one hit the deck of *Victorious* and the sheet of flame that followed. But British carriers had armour-plated flight decks so very little actual damage was done. Later, the body of the pilot, still clad in his ceremonial clothes, floated past the bows of *Euryalus*. It was a weird sight.

There was a long top secret signal about the forthcoming invasion of Japan itself. All ships were going to be refitted with extra oerlikon and bofors guns before the invasion started, as they would be giving close support to the troops landing and could expect heavy air attacks. The signal went on to say it was also expected that the Japanese would fight to the last man, woman, and child, in defence of their homeland and up to a million casualties were expected in the initial landings. I still remember that signal when people talk about the murderous guilt of those who authorised the dropping of atomic bombs on Hiroshima and Nagasaki.

The end of the war came. Half the BPF was to go into Tokyo Bay with the American Fleet for the official surrender while the other half, including *Euryalus*, was to go back to Manus Island to replenish, then go into Hong Kong and take the surrender of the Japanese troops there. The Japanese garrison numbered about 10 000 men, and the total force we could put ashore was about 600, composed of sailors and marines. The Japanese refused to leave their barracks when ordered to and the situation began to look very awkward. One Sergeant started to laugh and make obscene gestures towards the British surrounding the barracks. A Chief Petty Officer drew his revolver and shot him neatly between the eyes. From then on the Japanese couldn't wait to leave their barracks and line up in orderly ranks on the parade ground. It was also considered providential that the CPO happened to have been the pistol-shooting Fleet champion for three years in a row.

There was a company of Sikhs who had been prisoners of war since the Japanese took Hong Kong in 1941, and they had been badly treated. All of them were suffering from malnutrition, most of them from beri-beri, and some were blinded by the disease. We knew they didn't drink alcohol so we invited them on board early one afternoon to show them the ship. The cooks had gone to great lengths to provide an afternoon tea to be remembered, and the wardroom table was covered with sandwiches, cakes, tarts, trifles, and just about everything else they could think of as being in any way applicable to a tea table. Having shown the Sikhs over the ship we then brought them into the wardroom. A look of deep embarrassment appeared on their Colonel's face as he apologised and explained that this was one of their fasting days.

The civilians had been interned in Stanley prison on the far side of the island. During their four long years there they had literally nothing to do. Their food rations became less and less and the adults made great personal sacrifices to ensure the children remained as healthy as possible. And if there was any fun and games to be had, they had to make them for themselves. One of the inmates told me the Japanese commandant in desperation had a large notice displayed on the flat roof of the prison which said, 'Sexual intercourse on this roof is strictly forbidden during daylight hours'.

Almost from the moment we dropped anchor in Hong Kong harbour, the ship was surrounded by Chinese sampans. Something known as a 'gash' chute was always used in harbour to dispose of any leftover food, scrapings from plates, pots and pans. The Chinese used large nets to fish the 'gash' out of the water, then it was carefully laid out on the deck of a sampan to dry in the sun. After that, being much too valuable for the sampan people to eat, it was taken ashore and sold. There was a very sobering comparison to be made between their standard of living and ours, but I suspect very few of us made it.

We were back in Sydney in November for three weeks leave and I spent as much time as I could with Denise MacKellar. A few days before the ship was due to sail I proposed and was accepted. So far, so good. Grace, Denise's mother was also for it, so the one problem that remained was Denise's father. The legal age of consent was still twenty-one and Denise was eighteen. So we went to see him in his office in Castlereagh Street, in the heart of Sydney. We still have a picture taken by a street photographer as we walked down Castlereagh Street. Denise looks fine but I—wearing the white naval tropical rig complete with those sexy knee-length shorts and long white socks, and a white face to match—look like the Ghost of Things to Come. I felt even worse in the office when I stumbled and stuttered through a formal request for his daughter's hand in marriage. Keith had been gassed in the first World War and suffered from a nervous tic that would cause one eye to blink rapidly for some minutes at a time. When I had finished my stumbling request he stared at me coldly with one eye rapidly signalling in some kind of sinister private code. Right then, I would have vastly preferred to face up to Vincent Price in some torture dungeon.

'Don't be stupid', Keith said. 'She's far too young.'

The look on his face said he thought I was an idiot, and he did. He never changed his mind about me from that day on until the day he died. Somehow I managed to reel out of his office and by the time we got back down to Castlereagh Street I asked Denise what the hell we were going to do now. She seemed to be remarkably calm and suggested we go back to Cremorne and talk to her mother. Grace also received the news very calmly and said we shouldn't worry and, in any case, she had organised a party to celebrate our engagement that night. It certainly was a great party until Keith walked in unexpectedly in the middle of it, prompting in me a reaction that must have had a remarkable similarity to a coronary occlusion. The two of us retired from the party and spent the next half-hour with Keith enquiring about my future prospects after I left the Navy and me building a totally untrue picture of how my father had used his influence with Courtaulds to get me a job with them, and with the job went a cottage in the Cotswolds. Denise, who naturally believed the story, too, mentioned the job my father had got for me and the cottage in the Cotswolds that went with it in a letter to me some months later. The curse on all liars promptly descended. I then believed it implicitly and went around mentally thanking my father for all his good efforts until about ten days afterwards I suddenly remembered I had dreamed up the whole story in the first place. Anyway, Keith withdrew his objections to our marriage and the rest of the engagement party was enjoyed by all.

Early in 1946 *Euryalus* spent six weeks in Shanghai as the 'Senior Officer Afloat'. At that time China was being run by Ch'iang Kai Shek, but not very well. The Americans were very much around in Shanghai and becoming increasingly frustrated. They would track down former Japanese executioners and turn them over to the Chinese forces, only to be told to release them immediately because it was the job of the Chinese forces to track down former Japanese executioners and they would do it in their own good time. Once, when told to release an executioner, the Americans took him back to the Shanghai district where he had operated and released him in the middle of a crowded restaurant after having announced to the assembled Chinese diners exactly who he was. By the time the Americans reached the door, the executioner had been literally torn apart.

There was an RAF Wing Commander living in the British embassy ashore and I handled his signal traffic for him. His immediate boss was a Group Captain in Singapore who kept sending him increasingly desperate signals ordering him to take action on various matters. A typical reply from the Wing Commander would read something like: '*Your 231540. In my considered opinion your recommended course of action is both ill-advised and futile. I therefore am taking no further action.*'

One night at an embassy party we happened to meet at the bar and I found the alcoholic courage to ask him what the hell was going on between him and the Group Captain in Singapore. I suppose he was just drunk enough to tell me. He had been sent out to Hong Kong from England immediately the war finished and had thought there might be some chance of making money, so had transferred his capital of around £2000 to the Hong Kong Shanghai Bank. On arrival in Hong Kong he was given the job of flying a courier service from Hong Kong to Shanghai to Chungking then back to Hong Kong. At the time the Chinese dollar was very unstable and fluctuating wildly. The official rate of exchange was something like 700 to the pound sterling but any street trader would happily give you a rate of 2000 to the pound, or the equivalent to the Hong Kong dollar which was backed by sterling. So the Wing Commander would take Hong Kong dollars with him and exchange them for Chinese dollars from the street traders in Shanghai and take them to Chungking where Chi'ang Kai Shek had established his seat of government. For the sake of 'face' Chi'ang insisted the official rate of exchange be honoured in Chungking. The Wing Commander bought Hong Kong dollars at the official rate with his Chinese dollars and averaged at least a 100 per cent profit each time he did so. In the end, he said, things got too hot and they started searching both planes and pilots so the racket was finished.

It was a fascinating story, I admitted, but what did it have to do with his signals to the Group Captain in Singapore, exactly?

'I made just over thirty thousand pounds', the Wing Commander said. 'I'd like to get out and buy a pub somewhere in Devon or Cornwall. But I'm in the permanent RAF and they won't accept my resignation. So the only thing left is for me to get booted out'. He sighed happily. 'And you will agree I'm certainly doing my level best to achieve it.'

We went on a cruise to Saigon and Labuan. The troubles had already started in what was then still French Indo-China and we were told that a force consisting of French, Japanese and Gurkhas, was facing a rebel force across a river. After two days the Japanese, who were in the middle, had stopped worrying about the rebel force across the river and were standing-to facing the Gurkhas. Apparently, whenever there was a long lull in the firing the Gurkhas would get bored, shoot a couple of Japanese, then float their bodies downriver and use them for target practice. The Gurkhas had spent the last three years fighting the Japanese in the jungles of South-East Asia and they were not about to readjust that quickly, so the authorities wisely decided to send them to Labuan where they could rest up for a while and not shoot up people who had been suddenly upgraded in status.

Our visit to Labuan lasted five days and a good time was had by all. On our second day I was invited by a subaltern to go sailing in his dinghy with him the following day. It sounded like a healthy idea. We left at eight-thirty the next morning, threaded our way through the narrow passage in the tortuous reef for some two hundred yards and were then clear. The subaltern hoisted the sail and away we went for perhaps fifteen whole minutes, then the wind died completely. I had thought we were going to be out for a couple of hours at most so was wearing just a pair of shorts and had no cigarettes with me, either. Sometime around noon while we were still drifting away from the shore-line, we hoisted and lowered the sail energetically a number of times as a distress signal but nobody appeared to be interested.

The afternoon wore on and you could feel the sunburn increasing while the subaltern said he'd never known the wind fail like this before and the whole thing was bloody ridiculous but anyway they were bound to send out some DUKWs to look for us. I fervently hoped it would be soon because the coastline was beginning to merge with the horizon. The afternoon and the sunburn wore on and then the tropical night fell with its usual swift clang. About an hour later we saw lights on the waters as the DUKWs did indeed look for us. Only they looked about four miles short of our position and about a mile inshore of us. They seemed to give up very quickly and returned to the beach. I was beginning to wonder if South America was the nearest stopping point to Laubuan if we continued to drift the way we were drifting.

Magically, an onshore breeze sprang up. We hoisted the sail and eventually hit the outer edge of the reef. Joy was unconfined. Between us, we dragged the dinghy across the reef. One moment you would be standing in six inches of water and the next moment you would plunge into seven feet of water. But none of that mattered now we were no longer going to die of sunburn or old age while drifting down to South America. We got close enough to the beach to safely leave the dinghy and there was only one more shallow-looking pool between us and the smooth sand. I stepped into it happily, knee-deep, and my left foot descended onto something that squirmed violently and then began to arch. I screamed in stark terror and, I swear, jumped six feet into the air. When I came down onto the beach I saw the wing of a stingray break the surface of the pool I had just ejected myself from. We got back to the subaltern's tent and he filled two army mugs full of gin and vermouth in a 2-to-1 mix. I emptied my mug in about five gulps and began to feel a little better. The alcohol caught up with me about a half-hour later when we were trying to explain to the Brigadier that it wasn't actually our fault the wind had died on us and remained dead for the rest of the day. He was totally unsympathetic as was the captain of *Euryalus* when I got back on board later that night.

Innate sympathy was a very scarce commodity in the forces. I remember three weeks after D-Day, 504 was given a half-day off and told to go alongside a cruiser which we could actually board and have a hot bath. For the last three weeks drinking water had been the only water available on board the landing craft so the thought of a hot bath and a clean change of clothes was wonderful. So we came alongside the cruiser and boarded her only to be greeted by her First Lieutenant screaming at our skipper, 'Get this filthy scum off my clean quarterdeck'.

By the end of April we knew we were going back to Sydney again but this time we would spend five or six weeks in dry dock at Cockatoo Island. It seemed to be the perfect opportunity to get married, and we would have time for a honeymoon before *Euryalus* sailed.

We were married on the third of June, spent the first night of our honeymoon at the old Pacific Hotel in Manly, then had a week up in Mount Victoria in the Blue Mountains. If you were looking for a wild sophisticated time then Mount Victoria wasn't the place to look for it. Not that it worried Denise and myself. We had other interests—like the cafe directly across the road from the hotel which actually stayed open until nine every night. Dinner at the hotel was between six and 6.30 pm and it was too bad if you arrived at 6.35 pm. The middle-aged man who ran the cafe took a fancy to us—well, Denise, actually—and showed us how to gut fish and cook them along with steaks and various other things. The only prerequisite was a red-hot open range stove with a cooking space about far enough away so you could toss your steaks or fish onto it without getting spattered by the white-hot fat that inevitably resulted. My wild friend, Graham, had given us a dozen bottles of gin as a wedding present which we had taken on our honeymoon with us. Needless to say, there was never any problem in finding people to help us drink it. The hotel never actually said anything about it; they just refused to remove the empty bottles from outside the door. There were nine of them by the time we left.

Back in Sydney, Grace had tactfully gone to stay with friends for a while, leaving us the Cremorne flat to play house in. We entertained Charles Grice-Hutchinson, the navigator of *Euryalus* to dinner. To finish off the dinner I made cheese on toast (I can't remember why) delicately cut into thin slices. I deposited a plateful on the dining table, went back to the kitchen for something and when I came back again the plate was empty. Enchanted by my culinary success I made another batch and put that on the table. An act which Denise and Charles seemed to think was hilariously funny. Again back to the kitchen and again the plate was empty. With tears in their eyes, Denise and Charles assured me there was no need for me to make a third batch. It wasn't until a couple of days later I discovered they had been throwing each batch straight out of the window as soon as I had disappeared back into the kitchen.

'We both tried a piece first', Denise tactfully explained, 'but it tasted awful'.

My two best friends in *Euryalus* were both permanent navy. Charles Grice-Hutchinson had been made a Lieutenant-commander two years before he was due into the promotional zone. Before joining *Euryalus* he had been a fleet navigator for a destroyer flotilla in the Atlantic and had a DSO and bar to prove it. Graham was a Sub-lieutenant. He had formerly been in submarines, right up until the time the train returning him from an unofficial overnight leave in London was late arriving in Portsmouth. Graham arrived at the quayside to see the submarine flotilla moving down the Solent in line ahead. Without delaying for a moment, Graham jumped into a small motor launch and told the bemused coxswain to follow that submarine. By the time the launch reached the submarine it was already starting to submerge and its deck was awash. Graham made a frantic leap onto the conning tower and then hammered away demanding entrance. The Flotilla Commander was not pleased to see the third in line of his flotilla suddenly change its mind about submerging in mid-submerge, as it were, and the Captain of Graham's submarine was not pleased with the reason for it either.

Graham was an incurable romantic. About three days before we were married, Denise, myself, and Graham sat up all night in the Cremorne flat, talking and drinking. At around four am when I had gone to the kitchen to get us a fresh drink, Graham seized the opportunity to propose to Denise, asking her to run away with him right then before I came back into the room. I'm glad to say Denise declined the offer.

In Saigon, when all the officers had been invited to an official dinner ashore, but several, including me, couldn't go because we were all suffering from 'Montezuma's curse', Graham and I shared a cabin. He woke me up when he returned at around three am.

'Just wanted to say goodbye', he explained.

'Goodbye?', I muttered.

He had met the beautiful wife of a high-ranking French official at the party and they had both fallen in love at first sight. So they were going to run away together this very night and he'd only come back on board to pack a few things and say goodbye to me. I told him he was crazy and she couldn't be serious. Oh, yes, she was, Graham said; she gave me her earrings to prove it. Then he pulled out a pair of earrings complete with substantial-looking mounted diamonds. I spent the next hour trying to persuade him to change his mind. The thing that finally did it was when I reminded him Saigon was French territory and, once the high-ranking French official discovered his wife had run off with a British junior naval officer, Graham's chances of making it to the border without getting his throat cut first were pretty remote.

Later, in Auckland, Graham found the New Zealand love of his life and they ran away together one night on the ship's motorbike with her riding pillion. Unfortunately, the motorbike broke down a little way from the ship and Graham pushed it back because he didn't know anywhere else he could get the bike repaired for free.

Time ran out and *Euryalus* sailed again. Denise and I said our goodbyes, completely unaware that she was already pregnant.

*They say it's the biggest thing in a guy's life. Getting married, I mean. In England you couldn't get married after three in the afternoon but in Australia, because it's upside down, you could get married in the early evening which is real great for the guests because they can drink themselves under the table and then just fall into bed.*

*So we got married in this great little church in Cremorne. And there's an arch of swords for us to walk under as we leave the church. Like doing it in style, you know? Then the reception and a load of real boring speeches except for mine. While I'm holding them all spellbound I can see the bridesmaid looking at me, her bright eyes kind of adoring and wistful and I give her a kind of mental salute and say, 'Tough luck, Joy! But Denise and me are now legally hitched and there just isn't anything you can do about it, so you're going to have to eat your heart out in silence.'*

(This is absolutely outrageous! It's bad enough him invading my very private life, but Joy's only interest in me was as the man her best friend was marrying. Around three years later we were delighted to be able to attend her wedding to Paul Brown. They are still very good friends of ours. What the hell am I going to say the next time we have dinner with them? A.Y.)

*Then after the meal is finished there's dancing and everybody watching me and Denise leading it and showing them how it's done. And finally, Denise disappears to get changed out of her wedding gown into something different for the honeymoon. Zowie! And we're off in the car to the Pacific Hotel in Manly. Into the room overlooking the ocean but who is about to look over the water on their wedding night? Some kind of a nut, I guess.*

*Our good friend, Charles Grice-Hutchinson, has achieved a superb piece of organisation. A knock on the door and in comes a waiter carrying a bottle of champagne and two glasses. He opens the champagne, fills the two glasses and departs with a happy smile on his face. What the hell he's got to be happy about I wouldn't know, or care. We drink about half a glass of champagne and can't take any more. Well, it's been a long day and all and we're ...*

(That's quite enough of that! A.Y.)

*So we pour the rest of the champagne into the washbasin so the waiter won't feel real bad about it the next morning.*

*There was a song one time about magic moments. You've got to believe me when I say I was coming up to one right then. I don't have to spell it out, right?*

(Damned right! A.Y.)

*I mean, it's time to go to bed and there is my beautiful blonde bride starting to undress and ...*

(I'll kill the son of a bitch! A.Y.)

# CHAPTER THREE
## REJECTED WRITER

From Sydney, *Euryalus* went to Auckland and then to Pitcairn Island where only a privileged few got ashore as there was no harbour. A few magical days in Samoa and Tonga, where we fired a twelve-gun salute for Queen Salote's bicentenary and were also entertained at a magnificent feast which featured one-day-old roast sucking pigs. And finally back to Hong Kong.

Demobilisation from the Navy was being done in groups according to your length of service. It had looked as if I would have another seven or eight months to go before I was demobilised but it was suddenly accelerated. There had been a lot of changes in *Euryalus*, too. Graham had gone to another cruiser and Roy Wadley, another RN Sub-lieutenant and good friend of mine had also gone to another ship, as First Lieutenant. They were given the job of taking back to England all the RN deserters who had been rounded up by the police. One particular hard line case had been delivered to the ship by the police when, as it so happened, the Captain, Roy, and the regulating Petty Officer had all been ashore. The hard line case had appealed to another Petty Officer to be allowed to go to the naval base at Balmoral and pick up all his kit and the Petty Officer had said he supposed it was all right. So, as Roy found out to his chagrin an hour later, the hard line case having been brought aboard by a couple of burly policemen had been allowed to leave again all by himself minutes later. Roy could well imagine the reaction of the police if he rang them and explained what happened. In the middle of all the agitation the hard line case walked up the gangway complete with his kitbag and hammock and politely enquired the way to the cells. Intrigued, Roy later asked him

why he had bothered to come back when he had walked off the
ship a free man again.

'Well', the hard line case said, 'I wasn't worried so much
about my kit, it was my racehorse I was worried about. I just
wanted to make sure he was going to be looked after all right'.

The hard line case had been a Petty Officer himself and had
set up a grapevine for all intending deserters. He found them
jobs, preferably in country towns, or in the outer suburbs of
Sydney, and promised them protection so long as they didn't
get into trouble. For this, they paid him twenty per cent of their
pay. He also had established contact with the police and if any
of his protégés got into trouble he would let the police know
where to find them. In return, they let him alone.

'I've done very well, sir', he said modestly to Roy. 'Apart from
the racehorse, I've got a block of flats in Bondi and a wonderful
girl who I'm going to marry when I get back. They won't give
me more than eighteen months at most when I get home, so
I'll serve my time then come back to Sydney with everything
waiting for me and nobody can touch me again.'

I don't think Roy tried to find any moral in that story.

With the end of the war secret cypher traffic had virtually
disappeared so I had been seconded to the paymaster's branch
and the paperwork wasn't exactly inspiring. My demobilisation
group came up in early September. *Euryalus* was going to make
a lengthy cruise around Japan and expected to get back to England sometime in the following February. Denise, as I now
knew, was expecting our first child in March. It seemed a bit
much for the nineteen-year-old expectant mother to travel to
England all by herself, so her mother went with her. They were
due to leave Sydney in the *Dominion Monarch* in October. I was
put ashore in Hong Kong just before *Euryalus* sailed and after
spending eighteen months in her it was a little like leaving the
womb for the second time. A boring week followed in the Hong
Kong Club waiting for a ship to take me back to England.

I got passage home in a depot repair ship, *Rame Head*. She

was full of machinery which gave her bottom weight. A cruiser with all its guns and superstructure has top weight and rolls quickly in a rough sea. The reverse was true of *Rame Head*. She rolled sluggishly to port, hovered ominously at the end of the roll for what seemed a hell of a long time, then slowly straightened up again to repeat the process to the starboard side. Her fastest speed was around eight knots with the wind behind her. Three days out of Hong Kong she hit a typhoon and it took us three weeks to reach Singapore. There were five passengers in the wardroom, including me. I spent most of the daylight hours playing bezique with a padre who was a much better player than I was. We played a shilling a point and by the time the voyage ended I was owing him around £50 000. I did offer him an IOU postdated to around the year 2000, but he generously declined to accept it.

The ship spent one day in Singapore and stayed overnight in Gibraltar and, although these were the only two ports of call during the whole voyage, *Rame Head* took nine weeks from Hong Kong to Plymouth. Denise and Grace had left Sydney over three weeks later than I had left Hong Kong and the *Dominion Monarch* passed us, hull-down, in the Bay of Biscay and arrived in England two days before we did. My first sight of Plymouth Sound, a lump of mud rising out of the murky waters on a grey November morning, gave me a painful contrasting memory of Cremorne Point of Sydney Harbour with the sun shining strongly out of a cloudless blue sky, and made me question my sanity in returning.

We stayed at my parents' house in the beginning. A fairly small three-bedroomed house in Ilford, Essex, but only just over the border and really another London suburb. There was us, my parents, Denise's mother, and my cousin Roy, plus my grandfather all living in the house at the same time so space was at a premium. I had brought home from Gibraltar a case of fine Spanish sherry—Tio Pêpe—at duty-free prices, of course. Wines and spirits were almost unobtainable in post-war Britain and my mother—a great wine buff in her own right—achieved some family fame by adding sugar to her first glass of Tio Pêpe because it tasted too sour, and then using a third of a bottle to make a trifle. Denise, Grace, and myself found a house to rent in Streatham. It was a terraced house.

The winter of 1946–7 was the coldest for some forty years. Everything was rationed, including fuel, and the food rationing was more severe than it had been during the war. Our bedroom was warmed by a midget gas fire. At night, we used to pull the bed over close to the fire, up-end the mattress to provide a draught-break behind us and sit there feeling not warm but definitely unfrozen.

For a year before I went into the Navy I had worked for British Acoustic Films. It was an unglamorous subsidiary of Gaumont–British Films, and made 16-mm versions of 35-mm films. I had been employed in the sound recording department and the Government enforced my re-employment in my old job as it did for every ex-serviceman. So I returned to the recording department as a sound cameraman. I was, I suspect, the worst sound cameraman ever employed in the film industry. I had no mechanical aptitude at all.

It wasn't so much that I disliked the job; I hated it. But I had no other experience to offer any potential employer and the money wasn't bad. Five guineas a week in 1947 was quite a respectable wage. In the days before transistors, sound cameras were huge affairs with a six-foot bank of valves standing beside them. As you re-recorded a reel of film, you would hear the sound track from the amplifier and watch the track being photographed through a miniature telescope. Imagine being forced to listen to your favourite radio programmes for eight hours a day. Then imagine listening to the sound track of 'The Life Cycle of the Bumble Bee', which was probably a two-reel film, and you had to record forty-five copies of it. The only relief was when you were re-recording the company's old feature films, made in the 1930s, for film library consumption. Patches of dialogue here and there became precious. There was a whole series of comedies—films made from the classic Aldwych Theatre farces, most of them written by Ben Travers—featuring Ralph Lyn, who always played the classic silly ass complete with a monocle, and Tom Walls, who was the sophisticated roué.

In one film Tom Walls was trying hard to seduce a rich French countess.

'Come', he said huskily. 'Let us away to your château, where I may steep myself in the liquid beauty of your eyes.'

I liked that quite a lot.

And one where Ralph Lyn, driving his two-seater open tourer in the countryside, was hopelessly lost. He came upon a country yokel, wonderfully dressed in a smock and gaiters, and carrying a scythe over his shoulder.

'I wonder can you help me?', Lyn said, in his impeccable Mayfair accent. 'I'm trying to find my way to Little Upton-on-the-Twist'. (Or something similar.)

'Oh yes', the yokel replied, in the same impeccable Mayfair accent. 'Take the first on your left, second on the right, and you can't miss it.'

Lyn's eyes sparkled with delight; 'Oh, I say!' He was absolutely enchanted. 'Cambridge?'

'No', the yokel replied in his flawless accent, 'I've just cut my mouth on a bottle'.

Priscilla, our daughter, was born on 22 March 1947. Whilst she and Denise were still in the nursing home I found a flat in Ealing. In contrast to the rambling Streatham house, the Ealing flat was tiny; a bedroom, a living room, kitchen and bathroom. But it was modern, having been built in 1938, and its heating was adequate. Grace and I moved in and spent one evening unpacking. Having unpacked two-thirds of the crates we discovered we had completely filled the bedroom and half the living room. Fortunately we did have a bottle of gin with us we had been saving for an emergency, so we drank half of it, repacked everything and prevailed on the caretaker the next morning to allow us to store the crates in the cellar. Gin is very helpful in a crisis.

The summer that year seemed to be trying to make up for the winter that had gone before. We would get up around six on a Saturday morning, leaving Priscilla under Grace's watchful eye, and go down to the river to Kew and walk along the towpath to Richmond and back. With what I was earning and Grace's contribution we could just about manage to survive and a holiday was out of the question. A newspaper ran a short story competition with a first prize of £1000 which was an enormous sum of money then. I had always vaguely wanted to write and now seemed to be the golden opportunity. I wrote a heart-rending story about a henpecked husband who endured thirty years of misery and humiliation then finally murdered his wife because she had forgotten to put the usual apple in his lunchbox. It almost moved me to tears as I wrote it but not anybody else, apparently. The newspaper boasted it had had over 5000 entries and mine obviously sank along with the other 4995 that didn't win a prize. But the bug had got into me.

I kept on writing short stories in the mistaken belief that because a short story was shorter it was easier to write. I also made another classic amateur's mistake. I only sent them out to the best magazines like *Argosy*, *Blackwoods*, *The Strand*, and so on, and they came back almost as fast as I sent them out. Sometime later that year I read an article about writing for radio. It was a very practical article which told you how to set out your script and who to send it to at the BBC. I wrote a half-hour play, a comedy about a father taking his family on a boating holiday, falling down and banging his head then afterwards being mentally confused and thinking he was back in the Navy. The doctor advised his family to go along with it as the best way of coping with a temporary condition. Well, yes, it sounds really stupid to me, too, at this stage. I had a charming letter back from a gentleman at the BBC who said that, unfortunately, I had sent the play to the variety department so he had passed it onto the drama department and I would no doubt hear from them in due course. But he did think I had a definite gift for dialogue and perhaps I would care to drop in sometime and discuss it with him further. Would I!

He stood me a cup of tea in the BBC canteen, again praised my handling of dialogue, and said they would be very interested in any ideas I had for a variety show. These were the days of the great radio comedy shows. He lent me a handful of scripts of such shows as *I.T.M.A.* and *Much Binding In the Marsh*. When I read them I was surprised to find that no script raised even a smile, never mind a laugh. Lesson number one in writing something to be said, rather than read. I went home in a euphoric mood with an assured and glamorous future ahead of me. Denise and I had already been talking of returning to Australia. That was still fine, I told her seriously that night, only, if I became a famous BBC scriptwriter in the interim, we might have to delay our departure for a few years. She had nothing to worry about. The script was returned a few weeks later from the drama department with a standard rejection slip.

I had hoped to return by emigrating to Australia but the man at Australia House said regretfully, but with some logic, he didn't think there was any great call for sound recordists in Australia at the moment. We managed to scrape the fare together with parental aid from both sides and sailed back to Australia in April 1948 in the SS *Maloya*. The ship was crowded so men and women were separated into four-berth cabins. Chastity was enforced, or you had to choose your moments carefully and not waste any time. The ship took six weeks from Southampton to Sydney and being a passenger proved just as boring as it had during my navy days.

We stayed with friends for a couple of weeks when we arrived in Sydney, then found a holiday flat in Narrabeen. The Managing Director of the then British Acoustic Films had given me some letters of introduction to film people in Sydney. I was warmly received by them, given tea or coffee and a half-hour of their time and then when, in desperation, I raised the question of a job, they all shook their heads regretfully. Ealing Studios, after having made *The Overlanders*, had announced they were going to stay in Australia and launch a massive film-making programme. But now they had just announced that their overheads were unfortunately too high so they were pulling out altogether.

Having got the same answer from the last of my introductions I was wandering around Sydney feeling very depressed. Then I realised I was in King Street, and a neighbour in the Ealing flats had told me I must look up his friend, Colin MacDonald, when I got to Sydney and say hello. He was the manager of Consolidated Agencies and their office was in King Street. As it so happened I was only a block away so I went into the office and met Colin MacDonald. He was very charming, gave me tea or coffee, and a half-hour of his time. He also asked me what I was going to do and I told him about the negative future of films in Australia at that moment. Had I ever done anything else? he asked. I had once spent three months on the sales side for Gaumont–British, filling in for somebody else, I told him. It was a ten-weeks' exaggeration but I didn't think it would hurt, and two weeks didn't seem to be worth mentioning. He rang me the same night and offered me a job as a salesman with his agency which I jumped at.

I spent the next two years with them selling, or not selling, torches and bicycle-lamps, door hinges, hatpins, and optical measuring equipment. Consolidated Agencies was a small outfit employing around eight people and was a nice place to work. Friends offered us their holiday home in Collaroy and we moved there from Narrabeen. It was a small cottage right on the beach at Long Reef and the boom of the surf put you to sleep every night.

We had some good friends in Collaroy, especially Don and Pat Brewer. They were both New Zealanders. Don had been in the Air Force and was doing a veterinary surgeon's course at

Sydney University. We also had neighbours who were inclined to invite us to intellectual discussion groups. The husband drank, the wife didn't. So halfway through the evening the husband would furtively invite all the other husbands out to the kitchen for a quick drink while his wife pretended she didn't know what was going on. One dreadful evening the discussion was concerned with classical music. The husband having admitted the only song he had ever liked was, 'She had to go and lose it at the Astor', had then snickered loudly. For this, his wife totally ignored him with acid contempt, then turned to Don Brewer and, waving a nonchalant hand towards the piano, asked if he played. Don admitted he did. Would he play something for her and her guests? Yes, he would. The wife sat down, composed an expression of rapt expectation on her face and neatly crossed her hands in her lap. Don solemnly informed the assembled company he would play them one of his own compositions. He then started to play a wicked honky-tonk style piano. I wish I could remember more of the lyrics. But here is the opening verse and chorus.

> "Why do I suffer,
> Have to bear all this pain?
> Twenty-eight days
> And it's back again!
> I got those men—stru—ation blues!"

Needless to say we were never asked again to any of the intellectual discussions.

In magazine publishing there were the *slicks* and the *pulps*. The terms had nothing to do with the editorial content but simply to the quality of paper they were printed on. The *Saturday Evening Post* for example, was a *slick*. Australian publishers had found a great success with pulp novelettes, around 20 000 words in length, which sold for sixpence a copy. Westerns were most popular of all. I bought a couple and read them avidly.

I knew absolutely nothing about the American West but, as I read on, I became convinced these authors didn't know too much, either. One of the stories started on board a train and in the second paragraph, a character opened an 'intercommunicating companion-way door'. Right then I began to feel if I couldn't write any better than that I sure as hell could write faster. So I started writing a western at home in the evenings. The big problem came when it was finally finished. How was I going to type it? Denise and I spent four Saturday afternoons in Keith's office using one of the office typewriters. When it was finished we wrapped it neatly and sent it off to Invincible Press which was an offshoot of *Truth* and *Sportsman*, and published westerns and romances. A month went by and then a letter arrived from them. They had accepted the story and enclosed a cheque for £20, being payment of £1 per thousand words for the copyright and all world rights.

Suddenly the world was a wonderful place. After three years of writing and being rejected, somebody at last had actually paid me money for something I had written.

My God, I was a professional!

*They tied one end of the rope around the bough of a cottonwood tree and the other end made a noose around his pa's neck. Then one of them lashed out with his quirt, the wild-eyed mare leaped forward and his pa was left dancing on air. What they wanted was the old Bar-X Spread because it had the best water on the whole range and lynching Pa on a framed-up rustling charge was the first stage in their ruthless plan. But when Pa's son heard the news about the lynching he buckled on his gunbelt and prepared to ride out. It was their fault the range war had started.*

*In the saloon the kid who had just lost all his money accused the professional gambler of cheating. The gambler shot him dead with a derringer that had been concealed in his coat-sleeve and didn't give the kid a black cat's chance in hell. It was a fair fight the gambler said and the rest of them inside the saloon agreed with him because he owned half the town, had the sheriff in his pocket and was the fastest gunslick they had ever seen. But when the older brother heard the news about what had happened to his kid brother, he buckled on his gunbelt and prepared to ride out. He was going to avenge the death of his kid brother by killing that professional gambler even if he had to take on the sheriff and half the town along with him.*

*It was the day he was going to quit being a lawman and hand in his badge. He had just bought a small spread where he aimed on raising thoroughbred horses. The stage was getting into town at noon and bringing with it his future bride, a lovely and dewey-eyed innocent blonde/redhead/brunette. But the stage never arrived in town. So he rounded up a posse and went looking for it. They found the stage in the pass where it had been drygulched. The driver was dying, the shotgun and all the passengers were dead. The lovely dewey-eyed innocent blonde/redhead/brunette was missing. With his dying breath(s) the driver told him there had been four of them; their leader was a big man who talked soft and had a scar down one side of his face. They had taken the girl along with them, as well as the gold and the passengers' valuables. His gunbelt was already buckled on so he forked his bronc past the stagecoach and picked up the bandits' trail. All the time his fingers were itching with the urge to catch up with them so his long-barrelled Colts could clear leather and pump lead into their stinking hides. And also, of course, to rescue his lovely dewey-eyed innocent bride-to-be from a fate worse than death. It was important he didn't forget that ...*

Retribution, was the name of the game whenever you wrote a western. I guess it was good five-finger-exercise

*(What does he do? Type with one hand only? A.W.)*

stuff, like getting in the regular practice. The beginning of the long hard trail ahead with all the plots to be dreamed up, the words to be written, and the characters to be figured out. Especially the characters. The long years of discarding and refining, working up to the big one the whole time. The character who would have everything. He would be tough, witty, urbane, sexy; you name it and he'd have it. And then, at last I got him right. So all he needed was a name but that wasn't easy either. It had to be exactly right. But I finally got that exactly right, too ...

*Al Wheeler.*

(Maybe I should have left him as the guy who worked in the reptile house at the zoo by day and solved the crime at night by thinking about it while he stuck foreign stamps into his stamp album and his name was Charlie Cholmondeley. A.Y.)

# CHAPTER FOUR
## THE ONE-JOB-A-WEEK MAN

I wrote more westerns for Invincible Press and even one romance which they accepted. Writing it became a form of purgatory after the first few pages. The true and tried formula was boy meets girl, boy loses girl, boy regains girl. But what the hell happened inbetween time? In 1950, not a lot. Australian censorship was tight even then, and about to become even worse. So the first romance I wrote was also the last.

In a minor fit of insanity I decided that selling encyclopedias would somehow bring me closer to the publishing world. For some time Denise had been saying she wanted another child and I had kept on saying we couldn't afford to have one. So I generously made her a deal; if I could leave Consolidated Agencies and start selling encyclopedias, she could have another child. The deal worked totally to Denise's advantage. She became pregnant and had our second child while I couldn't sell encyclopedias at all. In the meantime I had had an interview with Ben Bennett-Bremner, publicity manager of Qantas Airways, who was looking for a writer. I thought the interview had gone all right but had heard nothing further.

The encyclopedia publishers employed women to canvas various suburbs, telling the unsuspecting housewives they were conducting a survey. Naturally, they would need the names and ages of her children and the name of the school they attended. This gave you, the salesman, a list of likely prospects. Take Mrs Smith who has two children; Kevin (aged 10) and Bruce (8). You ring her doorbell and she opens the door:

'Mrs. Smith?' You are gravely courteous.

'That's right.'

'I'd like to talk to you about Kevin and Bruce.'

'Nothing's happened to them?!'

'No, no.' You give her a quick reassuring smile. 'It's just that the school ... well, do you mind if I come inside so we can talk about it?'

The trick was to make as strong an implication as you could that the school, or the headmaster, had suggested an encyclopedia would make all the difference to her children's future without actually saying it directly. Direct selling requires the ability to see every possible sale as a personal challenge. I saw it more like some kind of a nightmare and resigned at the end of the second week. During my first week I had been interviewed for a sales job with a wholesale newsagents' suppliers and had my fingers crossed that might come off. But, in the meantime, I desperately needed to bring some money in. There was—still could be, for all I know—a place in York Street called the Bureau of Higher Appointments. The title was more grand than the jobs they offered. I went in and asked if they had any temporary jobs. No, the gentleman behind the desk said, they didn't have any temporary jobs. I was halfway towards the door when he spoke again.

'Mr Yates', he said, very smoothly indeed, 'have you ever considered the fact that there is no such thing as a permanent job?'

So he sent me for an interview for a clerk's job which I got and started work the following Monday. The job was with a famous wine merchants. At that stage they sold all the wine they could produce and probably could have sold it twice over. Customer relations was all important and my job was to keep the ledger that recorded the allocations made to various hotels throughout New South Wales. The first morning I was given a sheaf of invoices and the ledger. There was a huge front office open-planned, where the minions worked, and at the back were the beady-eyed executives' offices so they could see everything that went on. There was also a huge clock facing us. It was mid-summer and as a concession the male staff were allowed to remove their jackets, providing they were wearing a white shirt and tie. On no account were the shirtsleeves to be rolled up. Smoking was not allowed in the offices, either. The only way to get through the long day that stretched ahead was to work, I decided. About 10.30 am, I had finished the sheaf of invoices given me by the chief clerk so went back to him for some more.

'What's happened to the ones I gave you?', he asked accusingly.

'I've finished them', I said.

'All of them in the ledger?'

'That's right.'

'The last bloke took three days', he said. 'Are you some sort of smart bastard trying to do us all out of a job?'

I assured him I wasn't and he reluctantly gave me a much thinner sheaf of invoices and told me they had to last me until Wednesday. It seemed like the longest day in my life. Just how many times could you sneak out to the toilets for a cigarette without somebody calling in a doctor? Midway through the week I had an urgent call from the wholesale newsagents' suppliers. Would I call round that evening after I finished work. I did, and he told me I had the job but it was imperative I should start the following Monday. Life suddenly looked a lot brighter. I wrote the wine merchants a letter. I didn't quite have the nerve to hand in my instant notice on the Thursday as it so happened that Friday was a holiday.

The people I worked with at the wholesale newsagents' suppliers were very pleasant and efficient. After the first week I felt I could really enjoy myself working for them. In the middle of the second week I had a call from somebody in the Qantas staff department. He told me I had the job in the public relations department but it was imperative that I start with them the following Monday. Life suddenly looked like it had me heading for a nervous breakdown. I wrote the wholesale newsagents' suppliers a letter.

At Qantas I was classified as an Assistant Editorial Officer and

my salary was £750 per annum which put me into something
like the fourth year of Grade 4 in the staff department's grading
system. There were, as I now vaguely remember, something
like ten grades with six years to each grade. If no other promotion came your way, your salary was automatically increased by
around £30 per annum as you completed your year in whatever
grade and passed onto the next. It was a challenging thought
that I would reach the absolute top of the staff grading system
in only thirty-eight years' time.

After having had four jobs in five weeks I decided the fourth
job was one I liked and certainly wanted to keep. Where else
could I have had someone like Ben Bremner for a boss? Ben
was a wonderfully talented man with a completely mercurial
temperament. Qantas proudly claimed they were govern-
ment-owned but not government-run. Although this was obviously true I don't think the top hierarchy ever learned to adjust
to a Ben Bremner. Had he been working for a perfume company
he would probably have become their major shareholder and
retired a millionaire.

I had been with Qantas for three months when the Editorial Officer resigned and I took his place. Well, I did his work,
but I was on a six months' probationary period. At the end of
it a member of the staff department rang me and congratulat-
ed me, saying the appointment was confirmed and my salary
was increased to £825 per annum. A miserable thirty shillings a
week, I protested.

'But don't you realise', he said, in a shocked voice, 'it takes
you from the fourth year of Grade 4 to the third year of Grade 5!'

There was no answer to that.

I was still writing in the evenings and at weekends. As well
as for Invincible Press, there was Consolidated Press and Transport Publishing Company. This was my first contact with a
Horwitz company and in those days, although they didn't pay
quite as much as the others, they did pay much more promptly
and that was very important. They also often gave you a title

for the book and a pseudonym to write under. On the cover of a western I had to agree that 'by Tod Conway' had a little more going for it than 'by A.G. Yates'.

As time went on I also branched out into other fields than westerns. There was a horror series and a scientific thriller series—I wrote under 'Paul Valdez' for that one and still have a sneaking affection for Valdez, wherever he is. There was also 'Thrills Incorporated', which was: 'Fantastic adventures, but these stories of tomorrow are only one jump ahead of science ... you too can take a trip to the world of space ships and interplanetary travel ...' Short stories only were required for this magazine and strictly in terms of space opera. Very often, when the editor was running to a tight schedule he would have the artwork already done and hand you a picture, saying, 'Three thousand words and a title, old boy, and I do need them by Friday'.

One picture he gave me didn't allow a lot of scope as far as the title was concerned, I thought, so I called it 'Jet-Bees of Planet J'.

He took another look at the picture when I brought in the manuscript, then looked at the title again.

'See what you mean, old boy'. He nodded approval. 'Sort of self-propelled by their own farts.'

There came a time when he complained to me that the scientific thriller I had recently written wasn't that at all but was really an almost straight detective story. However, they liked it and were wondering if I would be interested in writing a series along the same lines, and Carter Brown was born.

Life at Qantas continued. My job was to produce *Airways*, the monthly magazine, and also a quarterly staff magazine. In one issue of the staff magazine covering an open day held for the Mascot staff there had been a 'Queen For The Day' competition. Heading the article was a picture of three smiling girls, the one in the centre wearing a fake tiara. The caption underneath read something like 'Winner of the "Queen For The Day" competition was Miss Smith (*centre*) who is flanked by the runners-up, Miss Brown (*left*) and Miss Robinson (*right*), who proved themselves to be willing and sporting losers'.

Unfortunately, and I missed it in the proofreading, the *s* in 'losers' had been changed to a *v* on publication. The staff department at that time was very Methodist-orientated and they didn't think it was funny at all. I apologised to both girls for what had happened and they said it was one of the nicest things that had ever happened to them. Ever since the staff magazine had come out, their social lives had increased enormously. (I am virtually certain they didn't say 'by leaps and bounds'.)

Our first son was born on 25 September 1951. We called him Jeremy Rowan. Priscilla also has Rowan as her second name. Charles Grice-Hutchinson had been her godfather and his full name was Charles Rowan Grice-Hutchinson. In 1949, not long after Mao's communist take-over of China a corvette, HMS *Amethyst*, had been trapped a long way down the Yangtze River and she eventually escaped of her own accord, her captain and crew displaying a great deal of courage, ingenuity, and determination. But before all this happened, the Admiralty decided to send HMS *London*, a cruiser, down the Yangtze to rescue her. There were Chinese gun batteries on both sides of the river. The Admiralty's decision seems in retrospect to have been both idiotic and suicidal. One can't help wondering if the pre-war syndrome of sending a warship to 'show the flag' and quieten down the natives didn't still prevail at the time.

Charles had followed his own road to Samarra. When he arrived on the Far East Station he learned that *London*'s navigator was well overdue for relief and return to Britain, so Charles volunteered to relieve him. *London* had taken a Chinese pilot on board to navigate the river but when the shelling started he panicked and Charles took over from him. A shell hit the bridge, killing some of the crew outright and mortally wounding Charles. He died about a week later in hospital in Hong Kong without ever regaining consciousness.

Changes occurred in Qantas as far as the public relations

department was concerned. The quarterly staff magazine became a monthly staff newspaper. In consequence another writer joined us—Boris Carone, who fitted perfectly into the manic department. Boris stood about six feet, three inches tall and was proportionately muscular. He was also remarkably even-tempered which was just as well. He had been in the army and also been a journalist. When he was telling stories in the bar he had obviously also been anything from a steeplejack to a deep sea diver. Even Ben Bremner's eyes would flicker with respect as Boris completed an even more outrageous anecdote than the one that had gone before. But everyone, within a certain framework of time, achieves greatness, and it was Ben Bremner who surpassed us all.

It was still the days of BOAC and not British Airways and they had a representative in Sydney. The current one at that time had ginger hair, a flowing ginger handlebar moustache and a very highpitched voice. He also had one joke.

'Well, here I am in the colonies, trying to civilise you chaps and just not getting any help', he would bray loudly. 'I suppose it's all those convict ancestors of yours, what?'

By this stage I was some kind of hybrid Australian but my sympathies were all on the side of the full blooded Australians who had put up with this twit for a long time with a good mannered grace I found very forebearing. Until the magical day when we were all gathered in the pub at lunchtime as usual.

'I say ...' the high pitched voice dominated the bar, '... somebody actually called me a Pommie the other day. I wonder if any of you chaps know the true definition of the word, what?'

'I can give you the true definition of a Pommie', Ben told him, in a mild voice.

'Oh, jolly good!'

'A Pommie', Ben said carefully 'is an Englishman who comes to Australia, marries an Australian prostitute, then drags her down to his own level.'

The handlebar moustache quivered frantically and Ben

couldn't buy a round of drinks for the rest of the week.

Qantas opened a direct route to South Africa in conjunction with South African Airways. Ben took a team of Australian journalists to South Africa for a three weeks visit and I took a team of South African journalists, plus two British, on a tour around Australia. We went to Canberra and met Robert Menzies who spoke effortlessly for thirty minutes in answer to the first question, then on to Melbourne. One of the highlights was to be a visit to the rocket range at Woomera. Unfortunately, with the Burgess/Maclean defection from Britain to Russia still uppermost in Australian security's mind, they were determined to prove to the Americans that they ran a taut security in their own country (as one of their members told me in Melbourne the day before we were due to fly to Woomera). None of my team of visiting journalists were going to see anything of national importance there, he said flatly, and especially anything remotely resembling a rocket. And he was right.

On our first day in Woomera we were welcomed by the mayor whose incredibly-glossy toupee kept on slipping down over one ear. He proudly showed us the sights of the town which looked like it had been prefabricated a couple of nights earlier and probably had. The highlight of the tour was a long drive out to see the sewage works which caused the doyen of the British journalists to acidly comment to the mayor, 'I must say in my many years of journalism I have often found myself in the shit but this is the first time I've actually been driven to it'.

Our quarters for the night were at the RAAF encampment and I pleaded with the Group Captain there to help me out. A charming gentleman, he laid on a lecture by a grizzled veteran who looked like he had been born under a mulga tree. The rocket range extended more than 3000 kilometres from Woomera and it was his job, whenever a launch was imminent, to persuade any nomadic tribe of Aborigines to move out of the way in case of any mishap with the rocket. It was a fascinating lecture and saved the day. The three Afrikaner journalists walked out of the room with slightly bemused expressions on their faces. Why bother?, was obviously their unasked question. A couple of days later one of them confided to me how much he admired the way Australia was dealing with its black problem. 'You're just letting them die out', he said wistfully.

We spent four days in the Snowy Mountains where the vast hydroelectric scheme was being translated into reality. Their publicity manager was an enthusiast and we seemed to spend all our time travelling in ancient Buicks through snowstorms to one seemingly-inaccessible place after another. Tom Hungerford, the author of that fine book *The Ridge And The River*, with a background of the war in New Guinea, accompanied us as a writer then working for the News and Information Bureau in Canberra. His laconic comments upon our status from time to time did help a lot to maintain a just reasonable equilibrium.

We spent one night at the base camp at Tumut. Dinner was finished by 6.30 pm, then someone told us there was a 'wet' canteen just down from the camp. Five stalwarts, including myself, immediately set out in the teeth of a howling blizzard and finally found it. What our informant had forgotten to tell us was it only served cold beer, spirits being banned on the Snowy. Having gallantly fought our way to the canteen we decided a cold beer was better than nothing. The canteen manager suggested in a whisper that if we liked to hang around while he closed the canteen, and walk back to the camp with him he would be delighted to make us some tea and toast. Right then, it sounded like a banquet and we thanked him gratefully. When we got back to the camp and the main canteen, he carefully closed all the curtains over the windows then produced a half-dozen glasses, followed by a bottle of Queensland overproof rum and another bottle containing a sickly yellow-coloured liquid. He then filled each glass half-full with rum and topped it up with the sickly yellow-coloured fluid. It's the only drink I've ever had in my whole life where I could feel the top of my head lifting as

I drank it. After a couple of these—and the hell with the tea and the toast—someone plucked up the courage to ask what it was we were drinking with the overproof rum.

'Fermented pineapple juice', the canteen manager said happily. 'She's been going for six months now and she's a beaut!'

We were spending the night in unheated huts but plenty of blankets had been provided. When I got back to my hut, not only was my head swimming but my whole body was on fire. I stripped off my clothes, threw the window wide open, then collapsed on top of the bed. About three hours later I woke up with my teeth chattering uncontrollably and my whole body blue with cold.

The tour ended in Adelaide and I returned to the Qantas routine of the magazine and the staff newspaper. Carter Brown novelettes were selling well and I had stopped writing westerns, horror stories, and scientific thrillers. I wrote a full-length Carter Brown which sold quite well even at the horrific cover price of two shillings. Stanley Horwitz wanted me to write more but there was no way I could write more and still do a daytime job. 'How about we guarantee you a weekly income against royalties?', Stanley suggested.

I liked working for Qantas but I had no real future there. The next job up belonged to Ben Bremner and it was very unlikely I would get that until he retired, and then no guarantee I would get it. The thought of progressing up the yearly graded salary scale was not exactly enthralling at the age of twenty-eight. So I signed a contract with Horwitz which was to last thirty years and which guaranteed me a weekly advance of £30 against royalties. It was a crazy contract, of course. One of the troubles in Australia then was that a lawyer who knew anything about literary precedent didn't exist. That contract lasted until we signed a new contract in New York in 1961.

The one person who didn't take kindly to the thought of me being at home from then on was Priscilla, who was now at school.

'I can't tell all my friends my Daddy's retired', she complained. 'They'll all laugh at me.'

The aim was to produce two novelettes and one full-length Carter Brown a month. I didn't always make it but one month when I had, the print run covering the three was 200 000 copies. The return of unsold copies came to fifteen per cent which was a bit higher than usual and Stanley asked me seriously did I think I was losing my grip?

In those days when Stanley's father was alive he was known as 'Mr Horwitz' within the company and Stanley was known as 'Mr Stanley', obviously for the sake of clarification. I once rang and asked to speak to Mr Stanley.

'Who's calling?', the girl on the switchboard asked.

'Dr Livingstone', I said, with a sudden flash of inspiration.

'Please hold on, Doctor', she said respectfully. 'I'll connect you in a moment.'

I am doomed with original jokes. Somebody in Qantas was once expounding on the virtues of the maternity wing of a city hospital. It even had a monument to maternity in the grounds, he said proudly.

'I presume it takes the form of a permanent erection?', I said wittily.

'Of course it does.' He stared at me as if I had suddenly lost my mind. 'It's made out of bloody concrete!'

Through most of the 1950s Carter Brown was thought to be daring. They had daring covers with half-undressed girls on them. Sex was actually mentioned and implied. 'Damn' and 'Hell' were probably the two most violent expletives I ever used at the time. I don't know why the pendulum swung so completely one way during that era and I'm sure CB was only a very small part of the reason, if any. But the various States all introduced their own censorship laws. Victoria was the most cunning; their laws held the distributor responsible. Two convictions for obscenity and he would lose his licence. There was only one paperback book distributor in those days and that was Gordon & Gotch. So, the practical effect of the law, was to make Gordon & Gotch the State censors and they, naturally not wanting to lose their licence in Victoria, became the toughest censors ever. Queensland wasn't much better. I had, I think, three books banned in Queensland. One of them had two quite violent murders and a fairly bloody and violent climax. The reasons given for banning the book was that in a discussion between the county sheriff and his wife in the last chapter it was implied they might have had sexual relations before they were married. You couldn't undermine Queenslanders' characters like that. Everybody knew they went to the Gold Coast only for the sun and the surf. Looking back it is laughable but it was very irritating at the time. I can remember a Gordon & Gotch censor seriously debating if 'My God!' was permissible as it implied a personal god and not necessarily the Christian God. 'Oh, God!' was definitely out!

During this time I saw a debate on television where one of the participants was convinced that anyone who read any book that contained any sex would be instantly converted to pack rape. Every time he said 'pack rape' his mouth seemed to salivate a lot and his eyes glazed over. Any debate over censorship is both fruitless and endless it seems to me but one interesting thing during this time was you could, for example, have somebody murdered by being hacked into small pieces by a carving knife and nobody would have worried. But if your hero ventured to put his hand on a girl's thigh you were immediately in deep trouble.

Towards the end of the decade it all quietened down again and seemed to be virtually forgotten. Perhaps the State governments had become bored with censorship, or bored with the pressure groups that had brought about the acts? So then began the slow liberalisation through the 1960s until censorship in Australia seemed to be virtually abolished in the early 1970s.

*I figured it was time I made a personal impression. What the hell? They'd had the manuscript for a week already and not a goddamned peep out of them. So I walked into the office, closed the door in back of me and leaned against it. She didn't even look up. Too busy reading some crap in front of her on the desk. I put a cigarette in my mouth, scraped a match down the wall beside me and lit the smoke. She went on reading. I puffed a couple of smoke-rings her way and her eyes watered a little but she still went on reading.*

*'Good, huh?' I said. 'I write better.'*

*She looked up at me for a moment and said, 'Get lost!', then lowered her eyes again.*

*'Horwitz in?'*

*'Not to you', she said, and turned a page.*

*I moved closer toward the desk and took a real good look at her. A blonde, her blue eyes still a little watery, but then nobody's perfect. Well, I naturally made an exception in my own case. She was kind of cute, all the same. Wearing one of those sack-dresses that always cling where they should cling. And, man! where they were clinging right now I would have loved to cling. You could have skied down those swelling slopes and, with their uptilted angle, probably made a record long-distance ski-jump. She turned sideways in her chair so the hem of her dress hitched up a little and I could see her knees. Her beautifully-rounded and cutely-dimpled knees. It was kind of unnerving. I swallowed a lungful of smoke by mistake and had a coughing fit. She turned another page.*

*'Honey', I said coldly. 'Writers like me don't grow on trees. If you don't want to lose me, you tell Horwitz I'm here and he'd better move his butt real fast or he's in deep trouble.'*

*'Don't interrupt me', she said. 'I'm right in the middle of one of the sexy bits.'*

*'I write better sexy bits than he does', I said confidently. 'Whoever he is.'*

*She flipped back to the title page: 'Somebody called Carter Brown', she said. 'The plot is lousy but the sexy bits aren't bad.'*

*'Hold onto your bra, kid', I told her. 'I'm Carter Brown.'*

'You?'

She stared at me incredulously for a moment then started to giggle. I figured maybe she had the seven-year-itch, or something.

'So now you know who I am', I said, as I dropped the butt to the floor and rubbed it out on the carpet, 'you can tell Horwitz I'm here'.

'Crazy!', she muttered.

'I can understand you being crazy about me, sugar', I said in an understanding voice, 'but we don't have the time for it right now. I have to see Horwitz or he'll be making a big mistake and losing a genius writer who ...'

'Crazy about you?', she snarled at me. 'It's you who's crazy! If you don't get out of here I'm going to call a policeman.'

'You'll call a cop?' I had to laugh out loud like, I mean, Chee! 'If you want, lover', I told her, 'I'll call the ultimate cop for you and his initials are A.W.'.

(I can't stand any more of this. As I remember at the time, Stanley's secretary was very competent and wore a twinset with pearls. A.Y.)

# CHAPTER FIVE
## CALIFORNIA, HERE WE COME

We bought a piece of land in a North Shore suburb that seemed to be up-and-coming at the time, called St Ives. Keith thought we were insane to pay £800 for it. The smart way to build a house was to subcontract it, I thought, and started another bout of self-inflicted nightmares.

It was a timber house and the carpenter was not only a first-rate craftsman but also completely honest and helped a lot. Towards the end of the building I remember one morning when the electrician and the plumber and the man who had come to sand the floors were clenching their fists to decide who had the first priority. I quietly backed out of the room and fled, and didn't come back for a couple of days. But we did finally move into the completed house in 1956. Priscilla went to High-fields School in Lindfield and Jeremy went to their kindergarten before he started at the Sydney Grammar Prep at St Ives. Highfields kindergarten didn't mind how young they were and Jeremy had started there just before he was three. One day an elderly gentleman happened to be passing the school and stopped and spoke to a little English boy in the front garden.

'I suppose you must be the youngest boy in school?', enquired the elderly gentleman.

'Oh, no, sir', the boy promptly replied. 'One of our chaps comes in a pram.'

Carter Brown was now being published by a small English publisher and also in Finland, but they were the only two overseas markets so far. Stanley Horwitz visited America and tried to interest publishers there. The only one who showed any interest was Victor Weybright, the President of New American

Library. He later sent Stanley copies of internal memos; one he had written to a senior editor, Marc Jaffe, cautiously suggesting CB could be worth publishing with some more Americanisation. Marc Jaffe was distinctly cold about the idea, saying in effect that anything CB could do, an American writer could do as well, if not better, so why bother?

(It would be fun to say this of course was the end of Marc Jaffe's career in publishing. The fact is he went right onwards and upwards and became the President of Bantam Books Inc. in New York.)

One other problem at the time was that Mickey Spillane (published by New American Library) was the greatest success of the decade, and the majority of publishers—like 100 percent of them—were looking for writers who wrote like Spillane. Stanley thought it was worth another try and I agreed to revise a book I had recently written. It became a complete rewrite keeping only to the bones of the plot, and off it went to NAL.

Some time later back came a reply from Victor Weybright. He would like to do the book, and two more, then review the situation. As Al Wheeler was the protagonist of the first book he thought he should also be the protagonist of the next two books as opposed to using any other CB recurring characters.

*(Weybright wasn't about to go second class! A.W.)*

I was over the moon, of course.

Our domestic life was far less bright. Denise had been through a complete pregnancy but the child, a boy, was still-born. About six weeks later we spent ten days in Melbourne and it was an almost perfect holiday. We stayed at the old Menzies Hotel and had a suite with a vast living room. There were three smash theatre hits on at the time and tickets were supposedly unobtainable. We got returned centre stalls tickets for all three by happening to walk in off the street at the right moments.

One day we had been out visiting friends and got back to the hotel around nine-thirty in the evening. The Maitre D knew us by then and suggested, as his late liquor licence expired in thirty minutes, why didn't we have dinner in our room? It sounded like a great idea. The room service waiter was a Czech, known in the 1950s phraseology as a New Australian, and he set up the huge dining table and seated us at either end. We needed a model railway train to pass the salt. We ordered the meal and I also ordered a bottle of imported wine, a reckless extravagance at the time.

'He'll open it, pour a little into my glass then ask me to taste it', I said to Denise. 'I'll tell him it's no good and to take it back.'

We had already enjoyed a very convivial evening up until then and the thought struck us both as hilariously funny so, of course, when the time came there was no way I could do it with a straight face. The waiter had a lot of problems uncorking the bottle and apologised. 'These imported wines have very long corks', he explained. But then he finally managed to free the cork from the bottle and thrust it under my nose.

'Yes, indeed', I said, trying to be helpful. 'It certainly is a very long cork.'

'*Sneeef* it!' he said, his voice thick with contempt for the philistine.

Stanley had given us an introduction to a friend of his, Rex Testro. As the apple fell on Sir Isaac Newton's head, thus establishing the laws of gravity, Rex had once looked at the card on the inside of his hotel room door that told him the times meals were served and other vital information and wondered why nobody had ever added advertisements to them. Local services, he thought, like a nearby hairdresser for example, would surely like to advertise their services inside the hotel. So Rex suggested to hotels that he would provide all their printing for free, in return for the advertising rights. Rex and his brother worked hard at the project and were very successful, not only in Australia, but also England, Hong Kong, and various other places. By the time we met them, Rex could happily boast that the sun never set on the Testro empire.

He invited us to lunch at what was then the newest hotel in Melbourne. When we had finished our main course Rex summoned the waiter.

'We would like a bowl of fresh strawberries', he said, 'and by fresh, I do mean flown in from Tasmania today'.

'Of course, Mr Testro.'

'And a bottle of cherry brandy and a bottle of champagne. By champagne, I do mean French champagne.'

'Indeed, Mr Testro.'

The massive bowl of strawberries arrived. Rex emptied the whole bottle of cherry brandy over them, then the champagne was poured. We solemnly selected a cherry brandy-soaked strawberry, dunked it in our French champagne then ate it. To say we were replete after lunch would be like saying Marilyn Monroe was an attractive girl. But we were by no means finished. Rex accompanied us back to Menzies and led us straight to the long bar. There was a row of liqueur bottles standing on the top shelf so we decided to drink our way through them starting with a drink from the first bottle on the left. The third liqueur was Strega and that slowed us down a little. Rex suggested he might make us a mint julep. It sounded like a good idea; even better, a respite while he made it.

'Barman', Rex said. 'Bring me three ice buckets full of mint.'

Without batting an eyelid, the barman produced three ice buckets full of mint. It took Rex around thirty minutes to build his mint julep and it undoubtedly was a work of art by the time he had finished. It was carefully poured into sixteen ounce glasses and drunk reverently. These were the days of the barbaric Australian six o'clock closing and by five in the afternoon the long bar, which was as I remember the longest bar in Australia then, was becoming very crowded. Rex checked his wallet and decided he was running short of money.

'Do you have a phone, waiter?'

The phone was produced promptly on the bar in front of him. Rex dialled his office number then said, in a voice that carried the length of the long bar, 'Testro here. I'm in the long bar at Menzies. Send me down a handful of banknotes.' Then he hung up.

Ten minutes later a nervous office-boy thrust a fat envelope into his hand. We already knew the barman and I had said to him in the beginning to put the drinks on our bill and ignore anything Rex said to him, knowing it would be the only small way we could repay his hospitality. Rex was furious and tipped the barman ten pounds by way of getting even. We said our thank-you's and goodbye and went up to our room. Now we had precisely a half-hour before we were due to meet a party of executives from a Melbourne printers who then printed CB, who were taking us out to dinner and the theatre. I felt more like dying right then. Denise was glowing and full of life and I almost hated her at that moment. For the first time in our lives, naive that we'd been, we had a whisky sour, and the cutting qualities of the lemon juice did wonders. We dined frugally, managed to stay awake through the play—well, Denise did—and they insisted on taking us to supper afterwards. Denise did have an added reason for staying awake. One of the executives had been recently divorced and had arranged the seating so that Denise was next to him and I was around four seats away.

'Do you play?', he asked meaningfully, as his hand rested on her knee.

'Tennis', Denise said shortly and removed his hand from her knee.

She had no more trouble from him for the rest of the night, or so she told me when we got back to the hotel.

*The Body* was the first book that was going to be published by NAL. I had written *The Corpse* as the second. On our return from Melbourne I thought I had a great plot idea and wrote *The Blonde* as the third. Victor Weybright sent a cable saying, THE BLONDE VERY EXCITING STOP WOULD LIKE TO MAKE IT SECOND BOOK AND THE CORPSE THE THIRD. It was a very exciting cable and Victor capped it later in New York when he mumbled

something about he must have been carried away at the time
he sent it. The publishing date for *The Body* was July 1958. I had
been writing stories with an American background for the last
eight or nine years. Now I was about to be published there it
seemed like a good idea to actually see the place. So we travelled with Stanley and Nan Horwitz, leaving in May.

Two years previously Grace Gibson, who was a highly successful radio producer, had approached us with the idea of
doing CB on radio. *The Carter Brown Mystery Theatre*. We made
the deal with Grace explaining she couldn't pay us anything
like the royalties she would like to pay us because the brilliant
adapter-producer, Maurice Travers, whom she had just managed to get to agree to do the series was so expensive. Maurice
and his wife, Laurel Mather, the actress, became very good
friends of ours during this period and still are. A long time later
I happened to mention to Maurice how Grace had told us how
expensive he was. 'She told me exactly the same thing about
you', Maurice said. 'She couldn't afford to pay me a lot because
of the enormous royalties she had to pay for Carter Brown.'
H'mmmm.

The series was devised so it could be played as an hour
straight, or broken into quarter-hour episodes. I used to introduce each hour episode: 'This is Carter Brown bringing you another ...' The trouble was I had a nervous stammer and standing in a studio facing a microphone with all those professional
actors and actresses watching, did absolutely nothing to help.
But, with a lot of judicious editing Maurice made it sound not
too bad. I think. I never have lost that feeling of sheer terror
when confronted by a microphone. Television in many ways is
a lot easier because you can concentrate on whoever is interviewing you and let the cameraman and the boom-operator use
their own expertise.

Maurice and Laurel went to England in 1960 and he became
a senior producer with the BBC World Radio service. On the
way over he had written a television script and sent it on ahead.

There was a letter eventually from the editor of the series asking if Maurice would kindly see him. It was sometime during May of the year and, having just arrived in England, Maurice was hoping for a quick sale of the script. The editor turned out to be a pipe-puffing gentleman who was also very deliberate in his speech.

'Let me say straight out, Mr Travers', he said, between puffs, 'I like your script and we shall accept it. However, I would like one small change in Scene I of the second act'.

He went on to explain the change he wanted. It was minor and Maurice happily agreed to it.

'Now', the editor added, 'when do you think you could let us have the rewrite?'

Today was Thursday, Maurice knew. If this had been Australian radio he would have said by nine tomorrow morning. But this was a different world and if he said that the editor might think he was going to skimp on the rewrite. Monday would sound reasonable, Maurice thought and was about to say so but was interrupted by the editor.

'Would September be too much to ask?', he wondered, between puffs.

The radio show ran for two years. There was a gap of about eighteen months then Grace Gibson sold replay rights to another network. The first cheque arrived from her for ten per cent of the fee received. As it so happened our contract with her hadn't covered replay rights. Stanley returned her cheque with a letter explaining the position and said we thought 15 per cent would be more reasonable. A return letter from Grace made it clear she was outraged at the thought. She had never paid more than ten per cent for replay rights in her whole life and she wasn't about to start now. In fact she was immediately withdrawing the sale and would never offer the C.B. series for sale again. She did withdraw it and she never offered it for sale again to our knowledge.

At the end of the war somebody in Admiralty had thought

it was a good idea to put all cypher officers automatically onto the naval reserve. When the Korean War started I managed to get myself transferred to the Royal Australian Naval Reserve. Sometime in the middle 1950s I received a letter saying there was an Intelligence course open to reserve officers and to apply if you were interested. I was interested and applied. There were about six of us who turned up at HMAS *Kuttabul* one evening a week. I made two good friends during the course, Paul Trimble and Reg Torrington. The course itself was fascinating but having completed it the interest began to tail off. It was my fault entirely. I began to miss the regular evenings and finally, by mutual agreement, the Navy and I parted company.

One wonderful evening when we arrived in the wardroom at *Kuttabul* we found a serving engineer officer at the bar, with a very disgruntled expression on his face. He was slightly hard of hearing so Paul asked him loudly what was his problem?

'I had a drink in that pub down in Woolloomooloo', he said. 'You know what it's like in there; always selling bloody raffle tickets. So I bought one to stop getting pestered. The next thing I know this woman's all over me screaming. I've won'. He shook his head ruefully, 'When the feller sold me the ticket I thought he said two bob for a *duck*'.

When we left for America in May 1958, Priscilla was a boarder at Abbotsleigh School. An idea she had been very enthusiastic about because her total knowledge of boarding schools had been gained from the Enid Blyton books at that point, and she was looking forward to midnight feasts, feats of derring-do on the rooftops, and membership of some exclusive secret society. Jeremy was still at the Grammar Prep in St Ives and within reasonable walking distance of it. So Grace would keep house for us while we were away.

This was still in the days of the Super Constellation which, however super it might have been, was still propeller driven. That meant it lumbered along the ground slowly gathering speed and, at the moment you were convinced it was never going to get off the ground, would painfully lurch into the air. The flight to Fiji took eight hours and was a daytime flight. The four of us had drinks, some lunch, some chat and then we were in Fiji. The flight to Honolulu took fourteen hours through a long night, with not a spare seat in the plane, and then having to still wait until around lunchtime before arrival. Even being presented with an individual *lei* didn't make us feel any better at the time.

*(A lousy variation of the oldest phonetic Hawaiian joke in the world. Wouldn't you know he'd find it irresistible? A.W.)*

We stayed at the Waikiki Hilton in rooms opening on to the swimming pool, or if you preferred the ocean it was just over the way. We had three great days there then flew on to Los Angeles. The Clipper couldn't fly at the last moment so there was a delay until they found a navigator who could handle a DC7B which was a very new plane at the time. It was nearly midnight when we left Honolulu and Stanley generously handed around his 'happiness' pills to help us sleep through the night. They were something very new at the time called valium.

It was the only time in our lives that Denise and I flew first class and it was also a free champagne flight and it would have been a pity to waste it. I don't remember going to sleep but I do remember waking up as the plane was circling over the LA airport. The back of my neck was pressed against the top of the seat while the base of my spine just balanced on the extreme edge of the seat. The rest of my spine had set rigid like an ironing-board. It was one way to fly, anyway, and I've known a lot worse.

We stayed at the Beverly Wilshire Hotel for a few days then hired a car and drove to Las Vegas where we stayed at the Sands Hotel. The hotel rooms were set back behind the casino itself. Bellhops ran a continual service with small electric carts between the two, carrying guests and luggage. If you ever tried to walk it they obviously suspected some commie influence was at work. The first night in the hotel we saw a superb performance by Sammy Davis Junior and the following morning Denise and I went down to the pool for a swim. Beside the pool was a woman around thirty-five, wearing a black one-piece swimsuit and a large black hat to match. Her fingers were covered with sparkling rings and one arm had bangles up to her elbow. She was also smoking a cigarette in a black cigarette holder that looked to be longer than her arm.

'Rod, honey', she screamed, as we approached the pool, 'I just gotta get into that beautiful water!'

Rod honey appeared by the side of the pool at the shallow end and the lady climbed onto his shoulders. He then carried her across to the other side while she puffed on her cigarette holder and emitted shrill cries of glee. When Rod honey deposited her on the other side of the shallow end she said it had all been just too fantastic and she was definitely going to have another swim later.

Before we left Australia, a friend of ours who was a professional swimming coach, taught us a technique for using in hotel pools. Like all good techniques, it was simple and it worked. The whole idea was to establish your superiority as a swimmer without ever actually having to prove it. You sauntered casually alongside the pool, suddenly turned and executed a perfect dive then swam the *width* of the pool using a rapid crawl stroke. It would only take four actual strokes before you reached the other side. You then hauled yourself out of the pool, gave a casual yawn and walked back to wherever you had been sitting in the first place. The one cardinal rule was never to repeat the performance more than twice during the same session, or people might begin to start wondering why you never actually swam a length of the pool.

From Las Vegas we drove up to San Francisco and happened to arrive around five on a Friday afternoon. Stanley was driving and we took one of the exits that brought us straight into the middle of the downtown traffic probably at its weekly afternoon peak. We knew the name of the hotel but couldn't remember the name of the street. One other small detail was we didn't have a street map of downtown San Francisco, either. Finally Stanley managed to turn off into a quiet side street which, being in San Francisco, ran sharply uphill. Stanley stopped the car outside a mortuary where somebody was polishing a hearse and went over to ask directions to the hotel. The car was a Dodge with a pushbutton automatic transmission. Stanley had left it in neutral but hadn't applied the handbrake hard enough. So, as he crossed the road, the car started to run backwards slowly. Denise and myself were in the back of the car, and Nan was in the front. I leaned across the seat and pushed the 'drive' button and we started moving forward again. When we had gone about twenty metres I pushed the button into 'neutral' and we started rolling back again. It was a great game and the three of us were enjoying it. Stanley suddenly saw what was happening and streaked back across the road, flung himself into the driver's seat and slammed on the handbrake. That struck the three of us as being even funnier than what had gone before. Stanley, having just saved our lives, was not exactly appreciative.

After a couple of days in San Francisco, Stanley and Nan went onto New York. We had discovered Denise was pregnant when we had reached Hawaii and now the hotel doctor said she should take it easy for a few days. So we spent the next five days inside the hotel until the doctor pronounced her fit enough to travel again. We drove back down the scenic route on Highway One to LA, spending a couple of nights in Carmel. This time we stayed in the Beverly Hilton. A nightclub tour gave us a great night out—five clubs, or hotels, in time to catch their act—and we got a cab back to the hotel from the last around 2 am. The driver was definitely chatty. It couldn't have been our accents that told him we were foreigners.

'Beverly Hills ain't what it's cracked up to be', he confided.

'See that house over there? That's where Lana Turner's daughter gave it to Johnny Stompanato.'

Five blocks later.

'See that house over there? Rich little old lady got her throat cut from ear to ear last week. Her maid did it for the jewellery.'

Another eight blocks later.

'See that house over there? That's where Bugsie Siegel got his. He was sitting there in the living room when they shot him through the windows with a submachine gun.'

And then the latent philosopher who lives inside every cab-driver came to the surface.

'Man!', he said, 'It proves one thing. If you're going to live in Beverly Hills, you got to pull down those shades at night'.

One of the grey areas of travel is that your friends at home, with the kindliest of intentions, give you the names of their friends who happen to live in places you are going to visit. 'You must look them up', they say, 'they'll love to see you'.

It's a game of roulette. They may hate your friends at home for forcing them into extending you hospitality. They may simply hate you at first sight—or you, them. We had an introduction from a good friend with Trans World Airlines in Sydney to his good friend with Trans World Airlines in Los Angeles. We rang them one night and they, wisely, came to the hotel to meet us. They were Dex and Midge Barrett and are still very good friends. How about we have dinner in the hotel?, we suggested. How about we go out to dinner?, they suggested. A three-course meal with maybe some Irish coffee afterwards, or straight coffee and a cordial, they suggested. I was beginning to learn the language. Cordial translated as a liqueur. So we had each course in the best restaurant or club known for that course. Small bonuses were thrown in here and there, like eating our dessert while Hoagy Carmichael sang and played piano.

I had never been to a strip club. We had to go to a strip club, I told Denise because it would improve my knowledge of American background and help me write better books.

'I didn't realise you were onto your second martini already', Denise said, in some oblique way. 'What strip club?'

'It so happens they're advertised in the newspaper', I explained, holding out the newspaper it so happened I had with me.

What you tended to forget is the average distance between A and B in Los Angeles is probably fifteen miles. The distance between the hotel and the strip club was about that. The cab fare was astronomical. Inside the club was a raised dais where the strippers performed. We were given a table for two, foolishly ordered a meal, and asked about wine.

'We don't sell it by the glass', the waitress said grimly. 'If you want wine you got to buy a bottle.'

We bought a bottle. It had a very obscure label and was possibly Portuguese. But the large sticker halfway down the bottle guaranteed the wine to be ten per cent pure alcohol. There were five strippers and it was a non-stop show. Four very young men with an average age of around eighteen were given a table that was set with one end against the dais. That meant the inner two guys were very close indeed. One stripper walked across the dais until she was standing directly in front of the table, then bent forward from the waist and started her formidable breasts oscillating in opposite directions. The young man nearest to her rotating right breast had to turn his head quickly to avoid being slapped in the face.

'Coward!', the stripper said scornfully.

I used that, of course, in a book called, with an original turn of phrase, *The Stripper* and Al Wheeler was the embarrassed recipient. Ho! Ho!

*(What's this 'Ho! Ho!' bit? You figure you said something funny? I have to make sacrifices to further my career the way you have to make sacrifices to further your career, like writing this crap. A.W.)*

Then we flew to Chicago where the book-plugging was going to start and where Jay Tower, NAL's Publicity Director, was going to meet us. The flight started off with a clear blue sky and brilliant sunshine. After that long haul between Fiji and Hawaii, Denise had become terrified of flying. She sat rigidly in her seat, not looking to her right or left, as the plane flew smoothly on without even one tremor. Everything changed abruptly about an hour out of Chicago. We ran into a fierce storm and the plane started leaping around like a two-year-old. The Captain told us only one runway was open at O'Hare Airport so we would be delayed. When you looked out of the window and the cloud cleared a little you could see a plane beside you, a plane above you, and a plane below you. I simply didn't want to know about what you could see out the other side. And I was also starting to feel sick. Denise was busy comforting the woman beside us who was starting to have hysterics, and also coping with her young baby.

'I thought you were scared of flying?', I snarled at her.

'Not when it's like this', she said happily. 'I mean, now the pilot and those other people up front have got to be concentrating, haven't they?'

## Fame at Last

'I thought you were a much younger man.'
(This was said to me when I was twenty-nine.)

'Carter Brown? I'm afraid I've never heard of you.'
(At last count this has been said by 3721 people. It is always accompanied by an expression of incredulous disbelief that anybody who looks as stupid as you do, could possibly be a writer of any description.)

'... and his hero, Al Wheeler, who is perpetually intoxicated by the tinkling sound of his own voice.'

(New York Herald Tribune mystery critic's review of
*The Body*.)
*(You should have told me. I would have got him on a verbal
mugging rap! A.W.)*

'Carter Brown? I used to read you a lot. When I was
much younger, of course.'
(The only answer to this is, 'I'm sorry your taste has
deteriorated so badly'. I always use it.)

'That Carter Brown is real cute. You'd never guess he
was a fag.'
This was said to Stanley Horwitz by a New York
journalist.
'But he's not', Stanley said. 'I know him well. He's married, with three children.'
The journalist nodded sagely. 'There's a lot of them
like that. Frightened to come out of the closet.'

'With Carter Brown, I thought we might be selling
dime novels for a quarter.'
(Extract from Victor Weybright's book, *The Making Of
A Publisher*. The quote is probably not word perfect
but I'm *sure* I remember the gist.)

# CHAPTER SIX
# I NEARLY DROWNED!

You have to believe me when I say we've met a hell of a lot of people who never became good friends, or even friends, of ours. They became brief acquaintances, boring ships that sank in the night and they probably felt the same way about us, or worse.

But these are the people you forget. So, no prizes for guessing Jay Tower also became a very good friend of ours. She had organised a publicity programme for the three days we were in Chicago, starting with breakfast the following morning with a columnist from the *Chicago Sun*. Even worse, breakfast was to be held in another hotel from the one where we were staying. I have always thought Moss Hart had it right from the moment he could afford it. He stayed up one night to see a sunrise and wasn't particularly impressed then, for the rest of his life, he never got up before noon. We arrived at eight-thirty at the other hotel the following morning and were grateful to see there was a large glass of orange juice waiting for us. I took one sip and realised it was *good* orange juice.

'This isn't straight orange juice, is it?', Denise asked shortly afterwards.

'Known as the "Governor's smile" here in Chicago', the journalist told her.

It wasn't good, it was great. I had a second glass then enquired about the contents.

'Pure orange juice, honey, wheatgerm', he said, 'and a double slug of gin'.

The worrying thing is I have never felt so good at 8.45 in the morning either before or afterwards. Later he gave us a guided tour around police headquarters. After seeing a bullet that had been removed from the brain of a woman who had been murdered the previous day, Denise decided, what with her delicate condition and everything, to beat a strategic retreat back to the hotel.

'I saw from your potted biography you're a Duke Ellington fan', Jay said, around lunchtime.

I had bought my first Ellington record when I was fifteen in Shepherd's Bush Market in London. A seventy-eight, of course, secondhand; 'Take the A Train' on one side and 'Creole Love Call' with Adelaide Hall putting in a wonderful wordless refrain on the other. From that moment on I was a devoted Ellington fan and still am.

'That's right', I agreed with Jay.

'He's playing at the Blue Note Club here in Chicago', Jay said. 'I've booked us a table for tonight.'

For a moment there I didn't dare believe it. But it was all true. Duke Ellington came over to our table and talked with us, bringing Billy Strayhorn, the immensely gifted composer and arranger with him—two of the most talented gentlemen it has been my good fortune to meet in all my life. We had to leave the club to do a television interview but went straight back again.

The following night was also memorable but for totally different reasons. One of the largest hotels in Chicago had a huge room where top line talent appeared regularly. Beside it was a smaller room with perhaps twenty tables. At one end of the room was a raised dais and that was where Jan Eigan sat and ran his night radio show. It went out live, coast to coast, from 11.30 pm to 1 am. His girl Friday, complete with a trailing mike, came up to the table to do each interview. I was there to be interviewed by him, of course. What didn't help a lot was he only decided which would be the next interview on the spur of the moment. So when you arrived, you didn't know if you would be his first interviewee, or the last, or somewhere in-between. We arrived at 11.15 pm and I ordered a gin and tonic. The show started with Jan Eigan interviewing Red Skelton. That

really set me up. How was I ever going to compete with Red
Skelton? While I was brooding about that I ordered another
gin and tonic. The fourth interview was with a Frenchman who
was extolling the virtues of Paris as a tourist Mecca. The French
gentleman inadvisedly made a joke at Eigan's expense and was
promptly decimated, and Paris along with him. I felt a definite
need for another gin and tonic. Sometime around 12.30 am the
girl Friday appeared at our table and thrust her handmike into
my face.

'We have here with us tonight a writer. Carter Brown, all the
way from Australia', Eigan said smoothly. 'How are you tonight,
Mr Brown?'

'Glub', I said fluently.

'I believe your books have sold millions of copies in other
parts of the world', the unruffled Eigan continued. 'Why is it we
haven't seen them in this country yet?'

It was a wonderful feed line and I was launched into the
plug for *The Body*, which would be appearing in July. Eigan was
kindness himself to me, figuratively leading me by the hand until the interview was finished. Right up until that moment I had
been cold sweating sober but when the girl Friday walked away
taking her hated handmike with her, around six gin and tonics
caught up with me simultaneously.

We flew to New York and arrived on a weekend. The Hor-
witzes had found a penthouse suite in the San Carlos Hotel on
51st Street. It even had its own terrace with a great view of Manhattan from it. The Weybrights came in for a drink early on the
Sunday evening. It was a pleasure to meet Victor and Helen for
the first time. The dedication in *The Body* had read 'Per Ardua
Ad Weybright', and I hadn't been kidding.

The following day we visited New American Library which
was then on Madison Avenue. We met Kurt Enoch who jointly
owned NAL with Victor, Jack Adams, Vice-President in charge
of sales, and Brad Cumings who was my editor.

Victor gave a cocktail party in his very elegant apartment in the same building where Jack Kennedy had also had an apartment. Among those present were Gore Vidal, Jean Ennis, who was the Publicity Director for Random House and Lee Wright who was their mystery Editor. There was also Captain Hugh Birch from Qantas who gave me a wonderful rundown on current Madison Avenue advertising jargon. A few samples:

'Why don't we run it around the block and see if the wheels fall off?'

'Run it up the flagpole and see who salutes.'

'Do we know what's around the corner? That's the essential sophistication.'

I used all of them, of course, in a book entitled *The Victim*.

There was an interview with a charming young lady from *Time* magazine, but they never used it. (Cancel my subscription immediately!) I did a radio show with a Chief of Police from upstate New York and he proudly claimed they were the only police department doing their mug shots in full colour at the time. To show how enterprising they were, he produced a sheaf of colour photographs showing the body of a fifteen-year-old boy who had been knifed to death in the school toilets. Up until that moment I had never known that much blood could come out of one body.

Stanley and Nan left for Europe. Stanley already had a deal set up with Gallimard to publish CB in France, and was hopeful of making a deal in Germany. We moved down from the penthouse suite into a room with its own small kitchen which enabled us to make our own tea and toast for breakfast. One side effect of the entertainment we were enjoying was the quantity of food we were consuming. American restaurant servings are always lavish and facing up to dinner after having had an enormous lunch took a certain amount of resilience. After a while we got smart and always had eggs Benedict for lunch. The times when we were on our own for lunch we went to a place that catered basically for secretaries and had a lamb chop, mashed potatoes and peas for around a dollar fifty. The only thing was you were not expected to linger over your meal.

Jay got me an invitation to a police line-up. I felt quite blasé about it; after all I had seen them in the movies. Real life was vastly different.

*(I figured we were all through with the westerns, so how come the cliché-kid has started riding again? A.W.)*

The main part of the hall was filled with police officers from various precincts, there mainly to see if any of the prisoners presented in the line-up were wanted in their own precincts for any other crimes. At the end of the hall was a raised platform with horizontal lines painted on the wall behind to measure height. The platform itself was floodlit, leaving the rest of the hall in comparative darkness. The Captain conducting the line-up sat in a raised chair, giving him an uninterrupted view of the platform, and spoke into a microphone. For the prisoner, it must have been like suddenly stepping out onstage, being blinded by the brilliant lights, then being spoken to by the disembodied voice of God. You could feel the general air of tension and see it in virtually all of the people who appeared in the line-up. There were a couple of lighter moments:

'What were you doing inside the apartment block, Joe?'

'Painting the hallways, Captain.'

'So why did you steal the gun?'

'Well, this guy left the door of his apartment wide open and I could see the gun lying there on the table. Hell, Captain, if I didn't steal it somebody else would have for sure!'

And:

'Where did you get this package from, Hank?'

'A friend, Captain. He asked me to keep it for him for a while.'

'What's your friends name?'

'I don't remember.'

'It contained heroin worth around thirty thousand dollars. Did you know that, Hank?'

'No, sir. I didn't figure it contained anything valuable at all.'

'Is that why you taped it to the underside of the toilet seat?'

We spent five weeks in the San Carlos Hotel. Jack Adams was always complaining about the visiting firemen he had to entertain.

'Like you get them the hottest tickets in town—*My Fair Lady* probably—give them dinner, drop them at the theatre and then they look all hurt and say, "Aren't you going to see the show with us?" I've only seen the goddamned thing five times already.'

To our surprise, Jack asked us out to his Connecticut home for the weekend where he and his wife, Mary, gave us a warm welcome and we thoroughly enjoyed ourselves. After having lived for about a month in the hotel, hearing a bird singing in the morning was a kind of unique experience.

Jay also invited us to stay in a small holiday cottage she and some friends owned out on the tip of Long Island. On the Saturday it was decided we would have a picnic lunch on the beach. It just so happened it wasn't the right day for it. The weather was hot and overcast, and there was a strong wind blowing. We all retreated behind a sand dune to have lunch and drank martinis with fine sand floating on the surface, and ate hamburgers with fine sand embedded in the meat. By the time we had finished I felt hot, sweaty, and yuk! A swim seemed to be the answer but nobody else was interested. We had swum before lunch and found there was a strong rip running parallel to the beach.

I headed into the water, swam about a pool's length out then noticed the rip must have got a lot stronger because the sand dune hiding the rest of the party was now some considerable distance away. Meantime, the martinis and hamburgers had congealed into a hard lump inside my stomach. I turned around to swim back to the beach and found I couldn't make any headway against the rip at all. Not being a strong swimmer at the best of times, I soon began to thresh around wildly. The beach was completely deserted and it was no use me calling for help because the dune they were sheltering behind was too far away for them to hear me by now. The hard lump in my stomach was beginning to turn into a painful cramp. So there it was, I thought bitterly, I was going to drown off Long Island and nobody would even know. But maybe the water wasn't that deep? It could be worth seeing if I could touch bottom. If it wasn't that deep it could give me some incentive to start threshing about some more. So I exhaled, let my feet drop—and stood up waist-deep in water. As I walked back up the gently-sloping beach I began to feel quite pleased the sand dune had been too far away for me to call for help.

Medical advice said Denise shouldn't fly back to Australia, so we went by train back to Los Angeles. Brad Cumings farewelled us at Grand Central. In those days you caught the Twentieth Century, which left around seven in the evening and arrived at Chicago around eight the next morning. Being summertime, it was still daylight as you ate your dinner in the dining-car while the railroad ran alongside the Hudson River.

The Super Chief left Chicago for Los Angeles in the early evening so we had a day to spend in Chicago. We went back to the hotel where we had luxuriated in a VIP suite a few weeks before and I happily asked to rent a room for the day.

'We're between trains', I hastily explained, and the desk clerk's eyebrows slowly descended again.

Victor Weybright had insisted we should stay at the Beverly Hills Hotel on our return to Los Angeles, and had made the booking for us. The Super Chief lived up to its expectations with its observation car, club car, bar car, and superb food. The only thing was it was far more expensive than I had allowed for. At that stage we had a bank account with a New York branch. The conductor explained it was company policy not to cash cheques but he would personally cash us a cheque for a small amount, say twenty dollars? By the time we arrived in LA I had exactly eight dollars left. I told the cab driver to take us to the Beverly Hills Hotel in a nonchalant voice, then sat with my eyes glued to the meter. It clicked past eight dollars while we were still on the freeway.

The Beverly Hills Hotel looks like a magnificent country club set in its own estate, with an impressive flight of stairs sweeping down to the driveway. The cab stopped and two bellhops appeared as if by magic. I grabbed hold of the nearest one and hissed in his ear, 'Lend me ten dollars!'

His face paled a little but he did lend me the money so I could pay off the cab. By the time we had registered and got up to our room, I realised it was a different bellhop carrying our luggage. When I tipped him I said I owed the other bellhop ten dollars.

'Don't worry sir', he said smoothly. 'It's already on your bill.'

It was like living in fantasy land. Denise went to the hotel's hairdressers and found Hedi Lamarr sitting in the next chair. One morning as we walked out of the hotel we passed Cary Grant and Robert Taylor in earnest conversation, and later saw Jeff Chandler exercising his dog. The Barretts invited us for a weekend at their house in La Cañada, which was set against a background of hills, a swimming pool, soft music playing throughout the house and Dex made his celebrated gin fizz for brunch. It was definitely 'Beulah, peel me a grape' time.

The Barretts also drove us down to Long Beach and came on board the *Oronsay* to say goodbye.

'My God!', Dex said, TWA man to the end. 'You mean you're going to spend the next three weeks stuck inside this thing?'

He was right. There was nothing wrong with the ship, only the passengers. They were not so much boring, but dead-boring. As the ship neared Fiji, we realised it was then going on to Auckland before it reached Sydney. This meant another eight or nine days to go. In converting our round-the-world air tickets to return by sea, we had a leftover credit which had to be blown inside the next twelve months. It was certainly enough to fly us back to Sydney. So we got off the ship at Fiji, drove across the island to the airport and flew home. All we had with us was a briefcase each as the rest of our luggage was still on board the ship. So when we arrived at Sydney Airport we determined to move quickly through customs although there seemed to be an incredible number of barriers in the way. But we somehow got past them and stopped beside a customs officer's desk. He looked at us idly then looked away again.

'You want to see what we've got with us, or not?', I asked coldly.

He looked surprised, 'Did you just get off that plane?'

'That's right.'

'You're the wrong side of the barriers'. He shook his head slowly, 'They're supposed to be foolproof'.

Coming home was coming down to earth again. NAL had agreed to do one CB a month from publication of the third book in November so it was back to the typewriter. A few years earlier, a friend of mine, also a writer, had said he'd found dexadrine a great help for keeping him awake and keeping his concentration going. I went on using dexadrine happily for years, sometimes working for forty-eight hours straight. It was like castor oil, I always thought, the after-effects were lousy but it did its job. I was surprised when it was banned and slack-jawed at the thought of people taking 'speed' for kicks. What the hell kick was that, staying up all night and pounding a typewriter?

The gynaecologist was keeping a very close eye on Denise and she had a routine appointment with him just after Christmas. He wasn't happy with his examination and told me to take Denise straight to Hornsby Hospital, and he would do a Caesarian operation later in the day. When we reached there, Denise was ushered into her room by a student nurse, undressed and got into bed, then I was allowed in.

'You might take these home with you', Denise said, handing me her underclothes.

'All right', I said, 'but I don't know what my wife will say when she sees them'.

For some reason I was put out of the room again. A few minutes later the student nurse looked at Denise dubiously and said, 'Will I ask your—uh—friend to come back now?'

Christopher Rowan Yates was born on 27 December 1959, and was six weeks premature. The nurses made a big fuss over him until they weighed him and found he was a little over seven pounds. He and Denise were allowed home about a week later but it was strongly suggested we have a professional nurse in the house for a few weeks, which we did. They had been home about three days when a friend of Priscilla asked her to go with them to Mona Vale Beach for the day. They brought her home in the afternoon and told us she had been hit by a surfboard. The beach inspector had suggested they take her to Manly Hospital but they had thought it better to bring her home, stopping at our local doctor's on the way. Tom Neville said she seemed to be all right, but to put her to bed and on no account give her any painkillers, and let him know if the pain got worse. It was then a late Saturday afternoon. The pain got a lot worse and we called Tom Neville. He examined Priscilla and said he would like a second opinion. It so happened that Lex Johnson, a top Sydney surgeon was visiting nearby in Killara and he arrived quite quickly. They both went into Priscilla's room and then Lex Johnson came out a few minutes later.

'I'll call the hospital from here and make the arrangements', he said, 'but I don't think we should waste any time, so you put Priscilla into your car and drive her there now'.

We were too stunned to even ask what it was all about. We drove Priscilla to the hospital and then waited. The operation took almost three hours and Lex Johnson came to see us afterwards. There hadn't been a bruise where the surfboard had hit her side but the impact had fragmented her kidney completely.

'But she's going to be all right?', we said, but Lex wouldn't commit himself.

For the next ten days neither doctor would venture a definite opinion but then, finally, they said yes, she was going to live. She improved enough to come home for a short time but there was a drainage hole that wouldn't heal so Lex Johnson performed an exploratory operation and obviously didn't like what he found. So Priscilla went into another hospital where Professor Lowenthal performed an extremely delicate operation. One of the kidney fragments had become stuck to the aorta, the massive major artery, and the body—to keep things aseptic—had run capillaries into it so blood could circulate through it. Professor Lowenthal successfully removed the kidney fragment without any damage to the main artery. From then on Priscilla made a complete recovery and finally returned to school. Her end-of-term report was quite good except for the comment from the games mistress. 'Priscilla', she said, 'appears to be quite listless and to have no enthusiasm at all as far as games are concerned'.

*What do you expect front a cop? I figure you're entitled to expect him to stick his life on the line for you like if he happens along when you're being mugged, or raped, or kidnapped, or whatever. And if some nut with a highpowered rifle is picking off passing pedestrians, you expect a cop to do something about it, and fast. My guess is the vast majority of cops will. A life-and-death area is a black-and-white area, but there are a hell of a lot of grey areas like gambling, prostitution, and drugs. Cannabis is a great example. These days it's beginning to look like Lenny Bruce was right when he said after twenty years of smoking pot you might finish up with a chronic bronchial condition, but that was about all. If you figure the time, money, and effort that cops have put into trying to stop people from growing, selling, and smoking cannabis, it's kind of depressing. On the other hand everybody knows heroin is totally addictive and kills. So, without being wildly melodramatic, the guy selling heroin is selling death.*

*I've heard some real interesting stories in my time about New York. Of course, the time there CB is talking about I was only a kid, just a couple of books old. But I figure the stories were true. Like the one about the Magistrate who spent a whole morning hearing evidence given by vice squad officers against prostitutes.*

'If I was to administer true justice in this courtroom', he said, before he recessed for lunch, 'I would convict every officer who has given evidence here this morning of perjury. I therefore dismiss every case I have heard so far'.

That didn't make him the popular magistrate of the week so they elevated him real fast into the Chief Magistrate's job which was primarily administrative.

Then there was the rookie cop who graduated from the Academy and at the end of his first week in a precinct was handed fifty dollars by a Sergeant.

'What's this for?', he asked.

'Just take it', the Sergeant told him.

Around six months later he caught a pusher redhanded on the street and brought him into the precinct house only to see the man walk out again ten minutes later.

'What the hell was all that about?', he asked the Sergeant.

'Now you know why you're getting your fifty bucks a month', the Sergeant said.

Then there was a police Sergeant who had been tipped off where to catch one of the main heroin distributors in New York and caught him with the evidence he needed. On the way to the precinct house with two other officers in the car as well as the Sergeant, the distributor took a bulky package out of his inside pocket.

'Here's twenty-five thousand dollars cash', he said. 'Why don't you guys just drop me off at the next street corner?'

So a cop's life can have a hell of a lot of pressures that never come the way of the ordinary citizen. I guess that's about all the point I can make. Fortunately for me I don't have the same problems because I've only got two basic interests in life; homicides and girls, but not necessarily in that order. I even get paid to try and take care of the homicides and, when the time comes I have to start paying for girls, I figure I'll hang up my jockstrap and start writing my memoirs.

(The story about the Magistrate is true. In 1958 he and a social worker were collaborating on a book about the drug trade and its social implications. The story of the rookie cop and the Sergeant were actual taped interviews which I heard at the time. A.Y.)

# CHAPTER SEVEN
# NEW YORK, NEW YORK

We were invited to the first Adelaide Arts Festival in 1960 and thoroughly enjoyed ourselves. Morris and Joy West happened to be staying in the same hotel and we saw a lot of each other. During one of the literary sessions Morris had made a point in discussion and was followed by a university lecturer who earnestly began his contribution by saying, 'As Patrick West has just said ...'

Well, at the time, there was Patrick White who had just published *Voss*, and Morris West who had just published *The Devil's Advocate*. It seemed a pity to waste Patrick West so we decided later on that night he obviously was the author of *Schloss*.

It was in the early 1960s that 'in' words became vogue. Worse was to follow with 'in' phrases. Surely the ultimate horror was when people started saying, 'at this moment in time', as opposed to 'now'. Morris and I used to occasionally see what could be done with 'in' words contained in one sentence. Points were given for obscurity. Our best effort was, as I remember: 'When faced with a dichotomy it is best to maintain an attitude of pragmatic ambivalence'.

The one-a-month CB kept me busy. We had started with six Al Wheeler stories then introduced the other recurring characters, such as Danny Boyd. Boyd was a private detective who worked out of New York—and as Tony Boucher, the mystery critic of the *New York Times*, said, he agreed with another character in the first Boyd book who found him 'fascinating, in a repulsive kind of way'. Then there was Rick Holman, who worked in LA but almost exclusively for the rich and famous in the movie business.

There was also Mavis Seidlitz, who started life as the dumb, but beautiful, secretary of a private eye called Johnny Rio. But then she somehow outgrew Rio and became a private eye in her own right. She mostly had a scientific approach, like if a bra-strap broke she knew something significant was about to happen. And she always found the right murderer for all the wrong reasons. She was very hard to write and I didn't write too many Mavis books. There was one where she met up with Al Wheeler and they wrote each successive chapter in turn. Switching from one character to the other didn't make me paranoiac; keeping the continuity flowing without having one character tell the other what had happened since they last met made me paranoiac.

Somebody in France made a movie based on *The Body* which I never saw but the money was very welcome. Back in the early 1950s I had written a book with a Las Vegas background featuring a comic, who was accidentally caught in the middle between two mobs who both blamed him for things he hadn't done. Bob Hope had just finished performing in Australia and I had him strictly in mind when I wrote the book. A friend told me he knew Bob Hope's manager—who was also his brother— very well. So I gave him a copy of the manuscript and off it went to Bob Hope's brother. End of story.

In 1960, Gallimard published the book and I felt vaguely an- noyed about it. Why did they want to throw in an old title when I, of course, was writing so much better now. The film rights were sold in Paris and we saw it in 1963 when we were visiting Paris, and it starred Fernandel. It was called *Blaque du Coin*, which my French friends say translates as 'Joke in the Corner'. And they snigger a lot when they say it.

After Priscilla's accident we moved to a house in West Rose- ville for a couple of years before we moved back into St Ives— the gypsy in us—into another house that was bigger than the first one.

There was one of those deadly legalistic points about an old right of way which ran straight through what we intended to be the tennis court and it took months to straighten out. Another longer trip to America was planned and so by the time we finally moved in it wasn't worth doing anything to the house until we returned. The whole interior needed to be redecorated and recarpeted and the previous owner had allowed for this in the price. So we sort of camped out in the house until it was time to leave for the States. Jeremy had a birthday party with around a dozen small boys in attendance. Over the birthday tea they filled their water pistols with ketchup and squirted it everywhere over the walls and the carpet. We smiled benignly as we watched them. Friends would come to play tennis on a Sunday and everybody would contribute to the meal. After it was over we would throw away the paper plates, plastic glasses, knives and forks, and stay relaxed. Later, when the whole house had been redecorated and we worried if anybody spilled red wine on the off-white carpet, we often thought we would have been smarter to leave it the way it was when we first moved in.

Returning from the Adelaide Arts Festival in a turboprop plane, Denise had asked me what all those dotted lines were on the fuselage. 'They mean Open here', I said, without thinking. Two-thirds of the way to Sydney, bright fat sparks started to fly past from one of the turboprops. Denise called the hostess's attention to them.

'Don't worry', the hostess, who had obviously flown with Shelley Berman, said brightly. 'I'm sure it's nothing but I'll let the Captain know just in case.'

If the Captain didn't already know we were in deep trouble, we thought. A whitefaced hostess reappeared at the front of the aircraft and studiously avoided looking in Denise's direction. Presumably, the Captain had suggested there were better ways for her to use her time. The propeller stopped rotating, the plane landed at Wagga Wagga Airport—a hive of activity on a Sunday afternoon—and later another plane from Sydney picked us up.

We took the family with us on the second trip to America. It was my first time in a full jet and of experiencing the exhilarating take-off: a slight nudge in the back and there you were airborne, as opposed to that dreadful lumbering lift-off of the old propeller-driven planes. It was morale-building. We stayed for four wonderful days in Hawaii, then flew on to Los Angeles. There, we met the Barretts again and also the Wests. Morris was putting the finishing touches to the play of his book, *Daughter Of Silence*. I bought a secondhand Buick station wagon; seven seats and everything electrically-operated. We drove the northern route across to New York. For the second time I missed seeing Hearst's majestic house 'San Simeon', because I was so sure we didn't need to book ahead. Wrong again! Then from San Francisco to Reno and on to the places with the wonderful names like Cheyenne and Ogalala. Through the Chicago loop and onto the turnpikes and then finally into New York.

We found an apartment on a short summer rental at the corner of Central Park West and West 86th Street. It was the top floor of a fifteen-storey building and was airconditioned. Brad Cumings was in England as NAL had just bought a controlling interest in an English paperback house which was to become New English Library. Jay Tower and Jack Adams were still around. Kurt and Marga Enoch entertained us to dinner.

At dinner with the Weybrights one evening there was just the four of us. The maid presented two whole ducks on a serving dish to Denise. I couldn't make any sense of it. There obviously wasn't a whole duck each. Then I saw Denise insert the carving knife into the nearest duck and it gently fell apart. The chef had carved both ducks then put them back together again. I was glad they had been offered to Denise first. Later Helen Weybright asked had we noticed how badly the ducks had been carved? She really would have to send her chef to summer school, she decided. Later I asked her to lay out social New York for us which she did with great expertise.

Owning a yacht put you into the upper bracket of New York

society because you were talking about a $200 000 investment. Anything that cost less was only a boat. Central Park separates the East Side from the West Side of Manhattan. In those days only the East Side counted socially. But it wasn't enough just to move from West to East because people would remember where you came from originally. The best answer would be to make an extended overseas trip then come back and settle on the East Side. With the proper attitude the only time you ever admitted to seeing the West Side was when you were on your way to catch the *Queen Mary* to Europe. We did move straight across the park from our West Side apartment to an apartment on East 72nd Street but, as we were only foreigners, we didn't count.

About this time I acquired my first literary agent, John Tiffany Elliot. John had been born and bred in Oklahoma and at the age of eighteen had decided to seek fame and fortune in Hollywood. After three years as an extra, and once having actually delivered a single line in a movie, John decided that there was a strong chance he wasn't the next Clark Gable, and moved into the agency side of the business. When we first met him, John was a successful agent and a typical New Yorker. Manhattan, of course is an island. There is the Triborough Bridge which is Manhattan's main connection to the rest of America. One evening John said very seriously he often felt he would like to go back to Oklahoma and see how it was now.

'I've often felt like doing it', he confided, 'but then I think God knows what lies the other side of the Triborough Bridge'.

Stanley Horwitz and Lyall Moore came into New York and we started to negotiate a new contract. Both Lyall and Maurice Phillips (now the Managing and Assistant Managing Director of the Horwitz Group, respectively) had started with Horwitz around the mid-1950s—Lyall on the editorial side, and Maurice as their Accountant, but he decided early on there had to be more to life than accountancy and has proved himself right.

Our apartment was in a large block on East 72nd Street.

Once when Jeremy had been sick, a Doctor Pectal, who lived in the same block, had very kindly come across and looked at him, then recommended a GP. One night I woke up with an agonising pain in my stomach which, if anything, got worse. Around five am I couldn't stand it any longer and told Denise to call Dr Pectal.

'How can I, at this time in the morning?', she asked, with what, in any other circumstances, I would have seen as irrefutable logic.

'Call him!', I screamed.

He arrived ten minutes later, asked three questions, prodded my stomach twice, and said he was sure it was a gall bladder attack. But as he happened to be a gynaecologist, it would be better if he got a surgeon to see me later in the morning. Meantime, he pumped me full of painkillers for which I was very thankful. The surgeon arrived later in the morning, confirmed the diagnosis and wanted me to go to the hospital the following day for tests. But I had another attack the following day so he put me into hospital and operated the same day. It was just as well because my gall bladder was about to turn gangrenous. Stanley and Lyall were due to leave for London so the negotiations came to a sudden stop. Medical insurance was something I had overlooked. The surgeon, knowing we were visiting from overseas, very generously halved his fee, but it was still $1500! The hospital was superb but cost a hundred dollars a day and I was there for twelve days.

Priscilla and Jeremy went to the United Nations School which was within easy walking distance. The classes were co-educational and half of the lessons were taught in French. A very different world from St Ives Grammar School Prep for Jeremy. One day he asked if he could have a tie-bar and cuff links because his girlfriend admired them. Later he invited his girlfriend and two other friends for dinner. From the way he had talked about his girlfriend we were somehow expecting a cross between Marilyn Monroe and Jane Russell. It needed some adjustment when we were introduced to a ten-year-old little girl. After they had gone home Jeremy remarked that the other little girl had enjoyed the steak they had had for dinner. With the price of steak being what it was, we said, we certainly hoped she had enjoyed it.

'It was the first time she'd tasted it', Jeremy patiently explained. 'Her mother and father are vegetarians.'

Stanley and Lyall came back from London and the new contract was then negotiated. The deal was finally concluded around three am in a hotel room. We had become great friends of Mike and Fran Avallone. Mike is a very prolific writer and is known as the fastest typewriter in the East. During the boom of gothic romances, Mike was writing them under about four different pseudonyms, one of them being Priscilla Dalton. I have a copy of one of the Dalton books which is dedicated to his three sisters of gothic writing, whose names are of course listed. They are all Mike's pseudonyms. Not many writers have this kind of panache.

There was a great television show called 'Pm East, Pm West'. It ran for an hour out of New York, five nights a week, and then a half-hour out of Los Angeles. I appeared on one show devoted to mystery writers and compered by Mike Wallace. Rex Stout was one of the writers on the show. He must have been then close to eighty with a wonderful beard like a thin Chinese screen. A great gentleman and a great writer. The producer of that particular show was Murray Burnett, who had written the play which provided the basis for the movie *Casablanca*. He and his wife, Adrienne, also became good friends of ours. At a dinner party at their apartment one night, one of the guests was a songwriter. He had just finished a stint, along with three other songwriters, on the 'Rosemary Clooney Show'. She was married to José Ferrer at the time and, according to the songwriter, always seemed to be pregnant when they were making the show, so they kept on trying to find new camera angles. The main job of the songwriters was to do the arrangements of the songs Rosemary Clooney would sing on the show. 'What we need for the end of this show', one of them said about halfway through the series, 'is an upbeat semi-religious number'. Nobody could think of one so somebody else suggested they write it. They did in about thirty minutes, our songwriter friend said, and called it, 'I Believe'. His percentage of the royalties from that one song came to a lot more than he had been paid for the whole television series.

Murray told a true story about how, when he had been a producer with NBC he had suffered sudden attacks of violent nausea for no apparent reason. A clutch of doctors could find nothing physically wrong with him and one recommended he see a psychiatrist. After a number of sessions it so happened Murray suffered an attack just before his weekly visit to the couch, and told the psychiatrist what had happened.

'Did you have an argument with someone before the attack?', the psychiatrist asked.

'Yes, as it so happens', Murray admitted.

'And you wanted to kill him?'

'Right', Murray agreed.

'But because you are a very moral man with strict taboos about violence, you suppressed the feeling into your subconscious', the psychiatrist continued. 'And it had to find an outlet so it found a physical one.'

Murray said he realised the psychiatrist was right and asked why he hadn't said what the trouble was in the beginning?

'Because you wouldn't have believed me in the beginning.'

Murray said he had to agree with that, too. There was a short silence around the dinner table then one of the guests asked if Murray had ever had any further attacks after the psychiatrist had told him the root cause.

'No', Murray said, 'now I get migraines'.

We went by train back to the West Coast and stayed the night at a motel near the airport because it was an eight am flight the following morning. The motel was almost empty when we went to our rooms for an early night. Unbeknown to us the air-port had been smogged in during the night so the motel was crammed full by morning. We just managed to get on board the plane with the hostess pointedly slamming the door behind us. Then we sat there for another two hours until the smog lifted. About an hour out of Los Angeles, three out of the four compressors went and the Captain expertly brought the plane down from 30 000 feet to 9000 feet. The oxygen masks had opened but not dropped. So we had to return to Los Angeles, first dropping a great load of fuel off Santa Catalina Island. It was midday when we got back to the airport.

Lunch was on the airline, we were told. It was just being served when it was announced our flight was ready and we should board immediately. Denise, already resigned to a watery grave, sat in her seat with a blanket wrapped around her head, not wanting to watch the fatal plunge into the Pacific Ocean she knew was going to happen anytime now. Christopher had Caspar the Talking Ghost with him. Talking toys were still quite new at the time. You pulled a string and Caspar said something. There was a choice of nine things he could say. This time he announced in a cheerful voice, 'I'm not afraid!'

He was definitely speaking for himself.

We arrived in Honolulu early that evening and found the Wests occupied the next bungalow to ours in the Halekulani Hotel. A couple of days later Priscilla developed Asian flu and had to be rushed to hospital by ambulance. Christopher followed her the next day, so our stay in Honolulu obviously became extended. I had to send a cable to Grace, saying we were delayed, and also to our housekeeper's family. The girl at Western Union sounded like she was Japanese-Hawaiian. The housekeeper's address was North Curl Curl, but we managed to surmount that all right. Then came Grace's address: 'Coo-ee-noo, Kissing Point Road, Turramurra'.

'Hubba-bubba?', the Japanese-Hawaiian girl whimpered. I was beginning to know just how she felt.

Back in Sydney the old routine was soon re-established. Denise had done some acting a few years before, and Charles Walmsley, an old friend of ours who had been a professional actor and producer, said it might be fun to do a play. I was a member of the cast until I realised they actually intended to play in front of an audience. The thought so petrified me I chickened out and twisted Charles's arm to play it for me. In the event, he only played it a little better than I would have. Of course, the audience did hear every word he said, which would have been a definite improvement on my soundless mouthing, I reluctantly supposed. The play was produced locally and was very successful. A church hall became available for rent and the Intimate Theatre was born.

It ran for about three years until the church hall was pulled down. A very bright National Institute of Dramatic Art student staged a very successful production of *A Taste Of Honey* there. His name was Jim Sharman who later directed such little-known productions as *Hair* and *Jesus Christ, Superstar*.

In early 1963 we were stunned to hear that John Tiffany Elliot had committed suicide. Later in the year Scott Meredith became my agent and still is.

We planned a trip to Europe in late 1963. For some time we had considered we were entitled to a family of four and thought of adopting a child. We had no chance of adopting an Australian child and, with the many childless families hoping to adopt, it would have been selfish of us to even try. From my navy days in Hong Kong I had a great liking for the Chinese, so we thought it could be possible to adopt a Chinese child. We were put in touch with St Christopher's Orphanage in Hong Kong and the Reverend Mr Osborne was delighted to help. International Social Services sent a representative to interview us and we were okayed as an adopting family. Canberra said as long as we adopted the child outside the country and in accordance with the adoption laws of New South Wales, we would have no problem.

The Reverend Osborne said if we came to Hong Kong on our way back from the European tour, we could select the child and take him/her back with us.

So that was settled. We thought.

We left in the *Oriana* in November 1963. As it was off-season the ship only took nineteen days to Southampton and stopped at a number of ports on the way. It was the ideal voyage. It came to an end just as you were starting to get bored. Commodore Edgecombe was the Captain—a man with a mordant sense of humour. The ship had been on the West Coast of America before arriving in Sydney. In San Francisco he had entertained the P&O agents to dinner on board. One of his guests admired the quality of the port he was drinking and the Captain asked the steward what port it was.

'San Francisco, sir', the steward promptly replied.

A few days later when the ship was entering harbour at Long Beach, the steward was told the Captain wished to see him urgently on the Bridge. When the steward finally arrived breathless, Commodore Edgecombe looked at him, and then said, 'And what bloody port is this?'

My parents met the boat train at Waterloo and we went straight to the flat in Bayswater that my English publisher had rented for us. Two hours after arrival we found one of the bathrooms was in a dreadful state and completely unusable. A half-hour later the toilet in the other bathroom wasn't working at all. The agent, who would have made a shark look sympathetic, said there was nothing he could do until the next day at the earliest, so we moved out into the London Hilton.

We decided to have a meal in our room there and my mother, having told us the heartrending story of how she had to stick to a rigid diet on doctor's orders, decided she would have a double beefburger. Seeing our startled looks she made the point that her diet-sheet didn't actually say she couldn't eat a double beefburger. She still applies her own peculiar brand of logic to dieting.

As the flat rental had already been paid, Denise managed to get it put into order by having an imaginary conversation with me, while she was talking to the agent, about the exact time the health authorities would come to inspect the flat. Next door was a children's kindergarten school which our bedroom over-looked. I thought it was quite pleasant, but Denise declared she would never spend any time on her own inside that bedroom. She didn't know why, she just had a strong feeling about it.

When we were leaving, Albert, the porter, was helping us down with our baggage. He approved of us for having made the agent do something about the flat, then said casually, as we were moving suitcases out of the lift:

'It was all them A-rabs fault, you know.'

A-rabs? I had to find out more. Albert didn't need much encouragement.

'They used to cook things on the bathroom floor. And then there was all that nasty business with one of the wives.'

The A-rab potentate had brought with him his Number One Wife, according to Albert, and his latest wife who was very young and very pretty. Number One Wife was now into late middle age and insanely jealous. So one evening she had sug-gested they might like tea and had brought it to the bedroom. She had also loaded the new wife's cup of tea with arsenic and the girl had died in agony in the bedroom.

'We had a lot of gentlemen from the Home Office here after-wards', Albert said. 'It was all hushed up, of course. They let the A-rab take his Number One Wife back with him and I expect he had her executed when they got there.'

It certainly seemed a good enough reason for Denise to have felt there was something wrong with the room.

*They found this head, long before my time, way back in the Thirties. A real good-looking guy with thick curly black hair, and dark brown eyes. The big problem was that was all they ever did find of him. No body, no arms, no legs; just his head. The guy was never identified and his murderer never caught. But somebody figured it would be a crying shame to waste the head. So they put it into a large glass jar of formaldehyde and stashed it in the crime lab.*

*If you can't help a fellow cop whenever you get the chance it makes you a real miserable kind of bastard I always figure. So whenever a uniformed cop gets upgraded to a detective I always like to give him his first look at the crime lab if I have the chance. At the right moment I always walk ahead of him so he can't see the jar. Then I grab hold of the jar, turn around fast and thrust it into his hands. By this time, of course, the head is bobbing up and down like it just can't wait to say, 'Hi, there!'*

*'Another one of your regular jobs from now on', I always tell the guy, 'will be to give it a shave every morning'.*

(This is a true story told me by a sergeant of the Riverdale, New York Police. There was no reason to believe he was lying and, besides, even Wheeler couldn't dream up a story like that. A.Y.)

# CHAPTER EIGHT
# FROM RUSSIA WITH MILK

We went through Europe by train. First to Amsterdam, where the hotel stood at the juncture of four canals. Watching the snow fall as we went up in the glass lift was a whole new experience. I think I was fifteen before I realised that song I had always liked wasn't, Two lips from Amsterdam'.

The Dutch publisher took us to lunch at a restaurant which had a tankful of live eels swimming around. You chose your eel and it was served to you in due course. Denise abruptly lost her appetite and settled for an omelette. When I was very young my father used to bring home a bag of live eels and produce an eel soup later, so I had no qualms. The publisher was about to stop publishing me. His problem was too many Dutch people had excellent English and they preferred to read CB in the NAL editions.

Two days in Brussels and then to Paris. We met M. Ribadeau Dumas, the producer of *Blaque du Coin*, the CB movie that was then showing in Paris. He worried if his English was good enough to use. It wasn't good; it was excellent. My schoolboy French was abominable. He took us to lunch at an excellent restaurant on the Left Bank. I vaguely remembered that *quel dommage* was the polite version of *merde*. At a moment in the conversation I sensed my chance to make my first joke in a foreign language. 'Quel fromage!', I said, and waited expectantly.

'That is very French', M. Dumas said approvingly. 'What a cheese!'

He drove us back to our hotel and on the way we passed the statue of Joan of Arc. M. Dumas pointed it out to us then added casually, 'You English killed her, you know'.

As it so happened Priscilla, in her first year at Sydney University, had written an essay on Joan of Arc.

'The real reason they killed her was because she believed in a direct contact with God and not through any intermediary like a priest', Priscilla said.

'Ah, well', said M. Dumas thoughtfully. 'You English did right.' In London we had met two very charming people from the Hong Kong Orphanage. They rang us in Paris.

They had heard from a good friend in Hong Kong that the law had been changed and now all orphans there had been made wards of the State. The gentleman now in charge of orphans apparently looked upon our prospective adoption with extreme disfavour for some reason of his own which we never did fully fathom. It was decided Denise and Priscilla would fly to Hong Kong, then we realised Christopher was still on Denise's passport, so I would go instead of her. Thomas Cook's had booked the whole European tour for us, so Denise, the two boys and the housekeeper would continue the tour and we would rejoin them as soon as possible.

It was the first time I had ever travelled alone with my sixteen-year-old daughter. We flew Air France and the air hostess—around thirty in age, but ninety in experience—brought the drinks trolley to a halt beside us and asked if I would like a drink. I certainly would, I told her. She looked at Priscilla and one eyebrow lifted into her hairline. 'And would, uh, madame, like a drink?', she enquired. I was about to say Priscilla was my daughter then thought it might well make things even worse.

We stayed at the Mandarin Hotel in Hong Kong and I got us two separate rooms to ensure we looked respectable.

We had a very unsatisfactory interview with the king of the orphans there. We were not suitable because we lived in Australia (!) and he also thought we were too peripatetic. Our chances might be improved if we were prepared to take two children, one of them an older girl. I said that was possible. Of course, one of them would have to be handicapped, he said. I spoke to Denise in Milan and we agreed that we would take two children, one of them handicapped if the handicap could be cured by surgery or therapy. It wasn't good enough for the king of the orphans. They would both have to be handicapped, he said, and he couldn't guarantee the handicap wouldn't be permanent. We were obviously playing the numbers game and he was prepared to keep upping the ante until we got tired and gave up.

Priscilla and I visited St Christopher's Orphanage in the New Territories and met the Reverend Mr Osborne. He was a wonderful Friar Tuck kind of man who obviously deeply loved all the children in his care. All the children were given English Christian names, as well as their own Chinese names. It was quite fascinating to meet a Chinese three-year-old who answered to the name of Victoria, and to wonder if she would ever find her Albert. We also met Andrew who, in spite of a dropped foot from polio, raced around as vigorously as the rest of them. The Reverend Mr Osborne suggested we take legal advice and we did. The lawyer suggested we come and live in Hong Kong. Private adoptions could still be made and that was the best answer.

We were to meet up with the rest of the family in Rome. I went to the Air France office to make our flight bookings. The very efficient Chinese lady behind the counter said there was a problem. My ticket was made out to Mrs Yates. I explained there had been a last minute change and I had taken the flight instead of my wife. It wasn't good enough. The Paris office had made a mistake, she said, and nothing could be done until it was rectified. I said, if it would make her feel any better I'd fly in drag. We argued endlessly and I realised I had just stepped on yet another of life's banana-skins. In the end I said I didn't give a damn what she did but I was going to board that plane the next day. Two hours later she rang the hotel and in a triumphant voice announced she had telexed Paris; it was definitely their mistake, and now it was all right for me to take the flight.

There was no direct Air France flight to Rome. So we would change planes at Tel Aviv and fly TWA to Rome. It was an afternoon flight, delayed for four hours so we finally disembarked in Tel Aviv around four am.

In the transit lounge a voice over the PA system said, 'Would Mr Yatz—or maybe that is Mr Yatezz?—please report to the reception desk'. Yatz, Yatezz, Yates? It was the confirmation of our TWA booking on their nine am flight. We had a cup of coffee and it was then around five am. I mentioned to Priscilla that we should take a quick look at Tel Aviv in the interim.

So we walked out of the airport building into pitch darkness and were standing around forlornly when a gentleman approached us. He was a customs officer, going off-duty for the weekend and wondered if he could help us. He found us a taxi in nothing flat then asked would we mind if he took a lift with us into Tel Aviv? Of course we didn't. On the way in he said he knew we were taking the nine o'clock flight out .and, if we were that keen to see something of Tel Aviv, the least he could do was show it to us. And so he did, magnificently. At the end, just before we dropped him in the city before going back to the airport he said, 'You know, of course, that it was Hertzog who said to the people of Tel Aviv that if you want a city you must build it yourselves'.

No, we confessed humbly, we didn't know that.

'But you're Jewish!'

We confessed we were not. He took this very bravely and later, of course, we remembered he would have also heard that 'Yatz—or maybe that is Yatezz?' announcement on the PA system.

The TWA flight was delayed three hours. When we finally boarded we realised for the first time it was going Athens-Rome. Just out of Tel Aviv the plane ran into a snowstorm and I had never experienced that kind of turbulence before. Priscilla lost her sense of balance completely and I was about to lose mine when the plane climbed above it. We landed in Athens and were told the snowstorm had shattered the plane's windshield, so there would be a four-hour delay. But they had lunch ready for us and had laid on a sightseeing tour. Consequently, at the time we were expected to be reunited with the rest of the family, we were standing on top of the Acropolis. Only air travel can do things like that to you.

We finally arrived in Rome early that evening. Denise had seen the Italian publishers in Milan. On their way to the hotel the young Cook's guide had been practising his English. The day before the Pope had just returned from his visit to the Middle East.

'Did you see the Pope on television last night?', the young man asked.

Denise said she had.

'He looked very tired'. The young man brightened. 'But then I think he had a very sexful tour.'

The next day was the last day in Rome as we had to keep to our schedule. One time in San Francisco, Anthony Boucher had asked me where we were going next.

'Well', I said, 'according to our schedule ...'

'You really say "schedule" and not "skedule"? He was mildly surprised. 'You know what Dorothy Parker said when she first heard somebody say "schedule"? "Oh, skit!"'

It was a beautiful January day in Rome, the sun shining and the temperature in the low sixties (the hell with Centigrade!). We hired a car and driver for the morning and he showed us the Coliseum and St Peter's.

Christopher had been fascinated when his grandparents had taken him to Westminster Abbey. He realised people were buried under the floor, so he had high hopes of St Peter's. His ultimate experience was seeing Lenin lying in state in Moscow. A real live dead body!

It seemed a pity to stop at midday when the driver was happy to carry on. Where would we like to go? Wherever he suggested, we said. He took us out to Tivoli and to Villa D'este, the

ninth-century home of the Pope with all its magnificent foun-
tains. We stopped for lunch at an inn high in the hills and ate in
the garden. There was a river flowing beneath us and a ruined
temple to Aphrodite standing above us. The driver politely said
he would wait and we insisted he joined us. We also asked him
to order the meal and it was superb. His bill was later presented
with the hotel bill and I noted he had carefully not charged us
his hourly rate while we were having lunch. A rare gentleman.

Three days in Venice, where the fog never lifted enough for
us to see the opposite side of the canal. We went to the glass-
works at Murano and the manager pointed out that, with the
quiet pace of life in Venice, people rarely died from heart attacks. Don't talk about spinal meningitis, he added. You could
see what he meant as you felt the raw damp penetrate to your
bones.

It was a ten-hour train journey from Venice to Vienna. We
bought excellent picnic lunches and with a two-litre bottle of
Chianti, Denise and I felt no pain—spinal or otherwise—at all.

The inevitable Cook's man met us at the station. With him
was another gentleman, who we later realised was the manager
in Vienna. He insisted in joining us for most of the time during
our stay and consequently we saw a lot more of Vienna than we
would have on our own.

One afternoon he showed us around a magnificent hotel,
decorated in the traditional Viennese colours. Then he took
Denise and myself to a wine cellar. It was crowded, so he sat
us down opposite a young couple who very obviously wanted
to be alone, and engaged the young man in a competition to
see who could drink wine from a full glass, without using their
hands and without spilling any. As we were about to leave, he
said would we mind waiting for him outside. He appeared some
fifteen minutes later and apologised.

'Did you notice the two young men sitting at the next table?',
he asked. 'They are wanted by the police and I had to do something about it. You see, I am also secret police.'

The next day he phoned and said the owners of the hotel
he had shown us the previous day would like us to have lunch
with them. We weren't too sure anymore, but Denise and I went
along anyway.

'Where are the children?', he demanded. 'You must ring and
tell them to get a taxi here at once.'

With more misgivings, we did. The owners entertained us to
a magnificent lunch in a private dining room and towards the
end of the meal our friend handed me a note. It read, 'It is in
order for you to tip the waiter 150 schillings'—no vast amount
at the then current rate of exchange. After that, he could have
told us he was Krushchev's younger brother.

It was a night train from Vienna to Warsaw. For some hours
the train ran through Czechoslovakia. The compartment was
invaded in the middle of the night by uniformed officials, including a big blonde lady who looked like she could swing
through the trees with Tarzan tucked under her arm with no
trouble at all. Denise had to get out of the lower bunk so they
could make sure she didn't have anyone hidden away underneath it. Then the butch lady gave me a pile of forms to fill out.
One of them was a currency declaration. I said reasonably that,
as we weren't getting off the train until we reached Warsaw,
there was no point.

'You will fill out the forms', she said grimly.

I filled out the forms.

An Intourist guide met the train in Warsaw and took us to
the hotel. We would like some information about tours, we told
her. There are no tours in winter, she said. The Intourist office
is closed. The hotel had an atmosphere of decaying grandeur
and it looked as if we were in for a fun four days. As in Russia, it
was the custom in Poland that a man was free to ask any woman
in the room to dance with him. One night in the restaurant a
young man asked Denise to dance. He stayed at the table with
us afterwards. He was a psychiatrist, currently studying the reasons for the Polish predilection for vodka. His wife was a singer

and he was waiting for her to finish her interview with Marlene Dietrich's manager somewhere in the hotel.

It was a long interview.

He sat in our hotel room until around two am drinking most of our last bottle of Scotch and becoming increasingly maudlin. That was the highlight of our visit to Warsaw.

When it came to paying the hotel bill I had run out of my smaller-denomination travellers' cheques and had to use one for £50 to make up the balance. I received back in change the rough equivalent of around £35 in Polish zlotys. They will change it into roubles for you when you reach Moscow, the cashier told me. They had a big laugh in Moscow over that story. Finally, back in London, Thomas Cook's gave me thirty shillings for my zlotys and they were being generous.

When we arrived in Brest, the Russian border town, the train had an official halt of thirty minutes. An Intourist lady, flanked by guards, met us in the carriage. She gave us a kind of welcome while the guards examined our passports. Then one of them spoke to her and her face looked bleak.

'He wants to know why you have arrived here by train when you were supposed to fly', she said.

'We were always booked by train', I said. 'Our visas were issued by your embassy in Canberra. We don't read Russian so we wouldn't know if they made a mistake.'

After a rapid interchange with the guard she told us all to put on our hats and coats and to go with the guards.

'This is ridiculous', I said. 'If we were always supposed to fly into Russia why are you here to meet us on the train?'

Another rapid interchange in Russian. 'The others will remain inside the train', she said, then pointed a finger at me. 'You will go with the guards.'

I was marched down the platform with two guards in front of me and two behind me, all of them carrying submachine guns. Inside, the station had a huge vaulted roof, reminiscent of a cathedral, and we walked past what seemed like half the population of Russia who were presumably between trains. Then up a flight of stairs and the Intourist lady gestured towards an empty waiting room. 'You will wait in there', she said, then followed the guards up another flight of stairs. The waiting room contained a batch of propaganda magazines in various languages, including English. I was just in the mood to appreciate them, especially after I heard the train pull out of the station. There was my family on their way to Moscow and God knew what fate awaited them there. Meanwhile, I would presumably take the direct route from Brest to Siberia. About an hour later the Intourist lady reappeared.

'Everything is in order now', she said, and returned our passports to me.

'Except the train's gone on to Moscow taking my family with it', I snarled at her.

'The train only pulled into a siding to wait for you', she said calmly.

'I will now take you to the platform where the train will return.'

'What was all that about, anyway?', I asked.

She shrugged at the naivete of the question. 'The border guards have their jobs to do', she said patiently.

I guessed there would be no point in asking what the hell kind of job it was they had just done. We arrived at the platform and I hoped the train wouldn't be too long because the temperature was around minus eight degrees.

'If you stand here', the Intourist lady said, 'in two minutes time the train will arrive and the carriage with your family in it will stop in front of you'.

She disappeared and the train arrived two minutes later at the platform. For the first time I really hated the lady from Intourist because the carriage containing my family stopped exactly in front of me.

We had dinner in the dining car later. A couple from the Thai embassy in Moscow, who were returning from Vienna, kindly translated the menu and ordered for us. The menu listed 'Tea with lemon' or 'Coffee with milk'. We asked for tea with milk.

'Nyet!', the waiter said firmly.

'Why not?', we asked.
He tapped the menu impatiently with one hand. 'It says "Tea with lemon" *or* "Coffee with milk."' He shook his head slowly. 'If you want tea, it must be with lemon.' He tapped the menu again. 'It says so here.'
We stayed at the Hotel Berlin which had been built in pre-revolution days and had vast rooms (our living room had a wildly-out-of-tune grand piano) with faded gilt and valuable pieces of Meissen pottery standing around. Our Intourist guide was a girl in her mid-twenties who once casually said to us, 'Shall we go up the applesand-pears?', then giggled delightedly at our reaction. A month before she had guided a party of London cockneys through Moscow and they had taught her a lot of their rhyming slang. It was bitterly cold in Moscow. One morning our guide sighed contentedly and said, 'I've just realised why I feel so happy this morning. The temperature has come up to zero'.
On another occasion she described a painting to us as representing the early communists.
'You can see this man in the foreground is telling the other slaves that they do not always have to be slaves', she explained. 'And the man in the background coming towards them is another communist who believes the slaves can free themselves.'

'Isn't the man in the foreground, John the Baptist?', I asked.
   'Yes.'
   'And isn't the man in the background, Jesus Christ?' 'Yes.'

'So it's a religious painting?'
   'Yes.' She nodded again. 'Now over here you can see ...'

Because there were six of us we were entitled to a car and driver for nine hours a day. One night Jeremy and the housekeeper were going to the ballet. They could have a car and driver to take them, but not to bring them back, the Intourist Bureau told me. I offered to pay extra for the car to pick them up. Nyet! But the Metro was very close and they would have to travel only one station back to the hotel. How would they know to choose the subway train going in the right direction? I asked. The Intourist lady said she would write it down for them, then all they have to do is show the piece of paper to anyone standing on the Metro platform. I guessed that was the best we could do and took the piece of paper.

I was learning fast. The first 'Nyet!' was the last. One thing the Russians obviously never did was to explain their reasons for doing, or not doing, something. Jeremy and the housekeeper returned intact from their night out.

'You didn't have any problem on the Metro platform?', I asked.

'Only with the first man', Jeremy said morosely.

'What happened?'

'Well, I showed him the piece of paper—he had a beard and he was wearing one of those fur hats—and he looked at it then said, "How the hell would I know, son? Why don't you ask one of these goddamned Russians?"'

Priscilla developed swollen glands in her neck. An ambulance delivered two doctors and a nurse. The swollen glands were due to too much exposure to the cold air, they managed to explain. Could they borrow one of Daddy's handkerchiefs to make a compress? They soaked the handkerchief in a colourless liquid poured from a bottle, then carefully knotted it around Priscilla's neck. She should stay in the hotel, they said, but there was no need for the rest of us to miss out on what had been organised for us. In the evening we should put a fresh compress on Priscilla's neck. It was important to soak the handkerchief thoroughly in vodka first, they explained.

The next day we arrived back at the hotel for lunch to find Priscilla missing. 'Do not worry', an Intourist lady said. 'They have taken your daughter to the hospital.'

Do not worry? We finally caught up with Priscilla in the hospital where they had given her tests and electro-therapy treatment. The medical treatment was first class and didn't cost anything.

On the day we saw Lenin's body the temperature was minus twenty-three and when the wind stirred in Red Square it felt as if your cheeks had been slashed with a scalpel. These were the days of the Krushchev thaw; Uncle Joe's body had been buried almost contemptuously outside the Kremlin wall and now it seemed even the Russians were telling each other what a tyrant Stalin had been.

We caught the overnight train to Leningrad. Priscilla was now allowed to travel but was to still have the compresses at night. One of my more stupid faults is never being able to resist the impulse to explain things when they don't need explaining. Ordering vodka late one evening from the barman (who spoke excellent English), I launched into a long explanation of how I needed the vodka to make a compress for my daughter's swollen glands.

'Of course, I understand', he nodded sympathetically. 'You wish for lemon and sugar?'

I could only hope my story rated as one of the more ingenious of all the stories he must have heard from various alcoholics.

We fell in love with Leningrad—its superb buildings, wide streets, and canals. And the Hermitage, that vast store of treasure trove. We spent three days looking at it. It would be easy to spend three months.

One day our guide marched us past a room mentioning idly that it contained the French Post-impressionists. We hastily backtracked and it certainly did contain a fantastic collection. But to her it was just another room full of paintings and you could understand that feeling from a professional guide's viewpoint. The Leningrad guide was also in her mid-twenties, married to an electronics engineer and they were both members of the Russian communist party, which is a rare privilege. She had been to Denmark and Sweden, translating at various conferences and was far more sophisticated than the girl in Moscow. Ergo:

'Carter Brown', she said, just after we'd met her and she asked me under what name I wrote. 'I'm pleased to meet you, sir. I have enjoyed your books very much.'

Oh, yes? 'Who was the main character in the books of mine you've read?'

'Al Wheeler', she said, 'and also Danny Boyd'.

It transpired she had read them in English from the library. I would have loved to know how they got into the library in the first place. She took us to see a palace of Catherine the Great's being restored and it was about an hour's drive out of Leningrad.

'Do you believe in God?', she asked suddenly.

'Yes', we said.

'My Grandmother believed in God', she said. 'Do you know how many people died in the siege of Leningrad? About two million. And a lot of them died from starvation. My Grandmother lost her husband and two of her children and many more of her relatives. And she prayed to God all the time. Did he help her, or any of her family? No.' She shook her head firmly. 'It is stupid to believe in God!'

Another time she asked us had we heard the story about little Ivan Ivanovitch in school?

'How big is the Russian communist party?', the teacher asked. 'Please, Teacher', little Ivan said, 'about five feet, nine inches'. 'How do you work that out?'

'Well, every morning at breakfast when my father has finished reading *Pravda*, he turns to my mother and says, "I'm up to here with the Russian communist party". And my father is five feet ...'

She showed us the Peter and Paul fortress where the political prisoners were kept. On the cell windows were shutters that when closed created total darkness inside the cell. No prisoner had been known in pre-revolution days to have kept their sanity after a week of confinement in total darkness. When the shutters were open the windows were frosted over so the prisoner could never see the outside world.

There was a niche in one cell wall to hold a candle until a woman prisoner killed herself by holding the candle to her throat while it burned through her windpipe. Nets were slung either side of stairways to make sure the prisoners had no chance of committing suicide by throwing themselves off a landing or from the head of a flight of stairs. The regiment who manned the fortress suffered as severe punishments as the inmates for any breaches of duty. Sometimes they would be staked to the ground outside the fortress and flogged. From a distance, the people used to say it would look like a writhing ant-heap.

From Leningrad we went to Helsinki and the train passed through the gap in the huge electrified wire fence that kills so many Finnish reindeer every year. For the last six weeks we had enjoyed being in Russia, but you found yourself breathing an involuntary sigh of relief when you crossed the border back into the West. It had a lot to do with being able to buy your own brand of cigarettes again and mundane things like that. But I still remembered being marched along that platform at Brest, not knowing at the time the whole thing would end in an absurd anticlimax.

We travelled overnight in an ice-cutter ferry from Helsinki to Stockholm. Then on to Oslo and Copenhagen, then another ferry to Hamburg. Denise had developed a sinus infection which had given her a painful ear ache. The doctor called by the hotel said that, as we were leaving the next day for Munich, Denise should see an ear, nose and throat specialist there. Meanwhile he had prescribed the best thing he knew to cure an ear ache—perhaps it was oldfashioned but his grandmother had sworn by it and he knew nothing better. Five minutes later a room service waiter delivered a baked potato. The doctor carefully cut it in half then offered one half to Denise. 'Hold this to your ear', he said firmly.

The appointment was made as soon as we got to Munich and the specialist, getting his nurse to translate for him, asked me to sit in his surgery while he examined Denise. He sat her down in a suspiciously-padded chair then got out what looked like the advanced version of a do-it-yourself Jack-the-Ripper outfit. He then extracted a long pair of narrow-shaped pincers with which he gripped Denise's left nostril, then deftly flipped her nostril inside out—or so it seemed to me the moment before I quickly looked away when my face turned green. Whatever it was he did it was successful, I'm happy to say.

We stayed there at the superb Four Seasons Hotel. One day we were having a pre-lunch drink in the bar. Two tables away from us sat two girls. One of them had long black hair and wore an ankle-length black dress cut in a very oldfashioned style. She was nothing less than a life-sized dummy! There was a dry martini on the table in front of her. The other girl beside her, also with a martini on the table in front of her was real, and not a dummy. They were joined by a second real girl and we couldn't help overhearing their conversation. Well, I certainly couldn't, not the way my head was tilted in their direction and my ears were straining.

The girl who presumably owned the dummy asked the girl who had just arrived what she thought about her (the dummy's) dress? The other girl said she didn't like it much. The dummy's owner said that was probably because she didn't have any taste. Both the real girls were Americans and speaking English, of course. My German is on a par with all the other foreign languages I don't speak. The conversation between the two girls became heated. Presumably they had a lesbian relationship and the dummy somehow figured prominently in it as an arbiter in many things, maybe only starting with fashion, and always to be quoted as an authority. Almost as good a gift as the torso-less head of the Riverdale sergeant's had been.

(What would have happened, I wondered, if someone had turned up in the crime lab some five years later, taken a look at the head in the jar of formaldehyde then said, 'My God! That's Charlie Oppenheimer!' So it became the start of an Al Wheeler story. The opening of a Rick Holman story was in a very elegant LA bar where he met the famous and sexy star who had a life-sized dummy beside her. Only this dummy was beautifully-dressed in the height of fashion and had very strong opinions of her own which the famous star kept quoting to Rick Holman.

There are rare days when real life bestows gifts on writers.)

We met our German agent, Dagmar Henna, who is now an old friend, and also met some people from Ullstein and Desch who were then both publishing CB. These days it is Ullstein and Heine who do the publishing.

One day we went and saw the village of Oberammergau then continued on to Ludwig's castle at Neuschwanstein. It was a perfect day; the sun shining out of a cloudless blue sky and virginal snow lying heavy on the bare branches of the trees and underfoot. The castle itself was a fantasy and perhaps the ultimate contrast to Elsinore which was built purely as a military fortress. Mad King Ludwig plunged his country into bankruptcy while he was busy building his wonderful castles, and they remain to enchant the generations that have followed him. Perhaps even bankers might approve of him now, but I suppose none of them thought of him as a good long-term investment at the time.

An overnight trip in the Orient Express took us from Munich to Paris. We arrived at eight in the morning, waited with our luggage for two hours for the Cooks's man to transfer us from one Paris rail terminus to another where we were taking the Golden Arrow train back to London.

From the moment you stepped on board the train you just knew you were back in Sir's country. Individual armchairs,

great food and service. Cooks had given us good advice and—
for an extra thirty shillings—we had the one cabin on board the
Channel packet. During the two hour English Channel crossing
we were waited on hand and foot. A special clearance through
customs, then onto the English half of the Golden Arrow and
the journey from Dover to London while you enjoyed the classic English tea served to you in your compartment, of course,
with the sandwiches, the large selection of jams and buns and
cakes, and the silver service. When you left the Golden Arrow,
it was not so much like leaving an old friend, but more like losing a whole way of life.

It's gone now, of course. It was losing money and British Rail
cancelled it so they could concentrate on losing more money on
other services.

*I was marched down the platform with two guards in front of me
and two in back of me, the four of them packing tommy-guns. We got
inside the station and there were like ten million Russians waiting
around to see some big football game, or maybe go invade someplace
they hadn't invaded before. Who knows? Who gave a goddamn, anyway? Then we walked up a flight of stairs and the Intourist dame
gestured toward a waiting room.*

*'In there, kid', she said, and walked up another flight of stairs with
the guards.*

*The waiting room was empty. I scraped a match across a propa-
ganda magazine and lit a cigarette. Checked my watch when I heard
the train pull out of the station. So that part of the plan was going
okay. Then the Intourist dame came into the waiting room and closed
the door behind her.*

*'Hi, Tamara,' I said. 'It was a great idea putting the border guards
onto me.'*

*'It was the best way I could think of getting us together somewhere
we could talk without arising anyone's suspicions', she said.*

*Tamara is a great girl and someday somebody's going to teach her how to speak English right.*

'You know he's dead', she said softly.

'Why, no, I didn't', I said. 'Hey! I'm real sorry, kid. I mean if he was somebody like real close and ...'

'They buried him outside the Kremlin wall', she said. 'It was in all the newspapers. Especially about him dying, I mean. '

'Oh, him!', I grinned at her. 'For a moment there you had me confused, kid. I figured you weren't talking about him, you know?'

She smiled wanly. 'Please don't do this to me, CB. You know English is only my fourth language. Speak plainly and clearly. I have other problems, also. I shall be thirty next birthday; I've been married for eight years and we still share a one-bedroomed apartment with four other couples. Most of the times I make love I don't even get his name right. The wheat crop has failed again and I'm wearing a bra two sizes too small and every time I breathe it hurts.'

*The way she was built I could see it would. Hurt, that is.*

'So they buried him outside the Kremlin wall, huh?', I said.

'There was nobody liking him very much when he died', Tamara said. 'They think there is a possibility that is why he died when he did. Because someone did not like him at all.'

'Good old Joe murdered, huh?', I saw the frigid look on her face and hastily added, 'I mean, bad old Joe was murdered, right?'

'They are not sure', she said. 'An autopsy was performed, of course. They could not find any poison but now they think there are some poisons that cannot be found, anyway. Are they not right?'

*It took me a few seconds to figure that one out.* 'Yes', I told her. 'They're not right.'

'They wish to be sure', she said. 'If it could happen to bad old Joe, it could happen to good old Nikita. You understand what I am conveying to you?'

'Sure, kid', I said, 'but why me? I've been wondering ever since that Czech bulldyke slipped me your note on the train. Is she strictly a business connection?'

*Tamara's face blushed hotly for a moment and she looked away.*

'It should be a beautiful relationship but someone—or something?—
always comes between us, but I should dummy up about that.'

'It doesn't faze me, kid', I said, 'but like I said before, why me? I
mean, the KGB hasn't gone out of business, right?'

'Please!', she shuddered prettily. 'Don't make jokes about the KGB.
In my country the walls don't just have ears, they have eyes and replay buttons for instant execution, too.'

'Okay, so no jokes about the boys', I said. 'But tell me because I
have to know and I'm getting real tired of asking the same goddamned
question the whole time. Why me?'

'It came from the very top', she whispered. 'The big K himself. It
appears he went to the library and got out one of your books. The
moment he finished reading it he called a summit meeting in the
Kremlin. He said there was just one person in the whole world who
could investigate bad old Joe's death and not only find out if he had
been murdered but also, if he had, find the murderer, too. "I tell you",
the big K told them, "this man is the most brilliant detective in the
whole world. He brings detection to the level of an inspired art. Not
only that; with it, he is witty, too, and also a great lover. We must
find him and bring him into the country immediately. Promise him
anything he likes in return. The complete female chorus from any of
our great ballet companies. Anything at all, but get me Al Wheeler",
the big K said.'

Tamara smiled ruefully. 'Then somebody had to explain to the big
K that Al Wheeler was a work of fiction. The big K broke down and
wept. "A tragedy!", he sobbed. "What is the loss of the wheat crop
compared to this?" So then somebody said we could get the writer of
the book, a guy called CB. "What does he look like?", the big K asked
and somebody told him truthfully. For some reason the big K started
sobbing again. "Get him, anyway", he said. "The way things are right
now with the wheat crop failure and all, I could use a laugh." So
that's how I came to contact you.'

Tamara's eyes glistened as she smiled at me. 'I have a personal
message from the big K for you. "Tell him", he said, "if he solves this
case I shall not only be forever in his debt but I shall make it well

worth his while in a very practical way". That's exactly what he said, CB.'

In spite of myself I couldn't help feeling a little intrigued. One of those golden domes from inside the Kremlin melted down for my own personal use, maybe? The possibilities seemed endless.

'Okay, kid', I said to Tamara, 'so tell me what the big K promised if I solve this case for him?'

'You're not going to believe this, CB', she said breathlessly, 'but tea with milk anytime you want it!'

# CHAPTER NINE
## THE HONG KONG CAPER

We took the *Queen Mary* from Southampton to New York—five days back in a 1930s atmosphere with a Palm Court orchestra playing in the vaulted dining room every night. I had picked up a virus infection just before we sailed and had to get a penicillin jab in the behind each day of the voyage.

I had a new editor at NAL whose name was Ed Doctorow. He was not only a very good editor but a very nice guy. He was also an outstanding writer, and still is. Among his other best-sellers, his *Ragtime* had a film made of it, and it reputedly earned him a million dollar advance. It seems sad in some aspects; I mean Ed had a nice steady job as an editor and he just threw it all away.

Kurt Enoch and Victor Weybright had sold out their interests in NAL and it was now owned by the Los Angeles Times-Mirror Group. Individual contracts for both of them had been part of the deal but they were both now being edged out into isolated splendour.

The housekeeper had flown back home from London. Now it was Priscilla and Jeremy's turn to fly back to university and school respectively. Denise, Christopher, and myself took the train to San Francisco, had dinner with Tony Boucher and his wife—organised by a collect telegram, the only way I could send it from the train—and boarded the *President Roosevelt* the next day. It was a cruise ship calling at Honolulu, then Taiwan, and Hong Kong. Most of the passengers were elderly widows, obviously spending the insurance money and out to have a ball. As we had the four-year-old Christopher with us, we were first sitting at all meals. This worked well in the evenings because there was an organised playtime for the kids on board after the first sitting dinner, and that meant we could have a drink comfortably in the nearly-deserted bar while the bulk of the passengers were at the second sitting.

One night a lady who could have easily passed for Whistler's mother, came moving very slowly through the bar on her way to the second sitting. She looked so frail and fragile that both Denise and I got to our feet to see if we could possibly help her. But then she suddenly slumped into a chair.

'God! I'm loaded!', she announced.

After about five minutes her eyes came back into focus, she hauled herself up onto her feet and determinedly continued on her way to the second sitting for dinner.

During the day the ship spent in Honolulu I bought myself some smart white swimming trunks. They gave me a jockstrap along with the trunks. I stopped wondering why the first time I wore the trunks (without the jockstrap underneath) when we went swimming at Shek-O beach in Hong Kong. When wet, the trunks became completely transparent. Slinking furtively back up the beach I realised I had just stepped onto another of life's banana skins.

But what must be close to the ultimate banana skin was stepped on by one of Stanley Horwitz's friends back in the early 1950s.

He and his wife were on holiday from northern Queensland and enjoying Sydney. One evening they went with friends to the Prince Edward, one of the last great rococo cinemas built in the 1930s; progress has now replaced it with a lyrical office block. It was the time when men were bidding farewell to fly buttons and Stanley's friend was wearing his first suit with a zip fly. During the interval he made a routine visit and when he re-joined their friends his wife hissed into his ear he had forgotten to zip up his fly. It was not the moment in the crowded foyer to do anything about it, he decided, but then the obvious answer occurred to him. At the moment the lights went out inside the theatre before the main feature started, he would rise quickly to his feet, zip up his fly in the darkness, then sit down again.

They returned to their seats and the lights went out. He got up to his feet and quickly zipped up his fly. Sitting in the seat directly in front of him was a girl with a ponytail which got caught in his zipper and jammed it. The main feature started while he was still frantically trying to free his zipper. Cries of 'Sit down!' came from annoyed patrons sitting behind him. The girl started to turn her head to see what all the commotion was about and found she couldn't turn it. An usherette came rushing along to see what the trouble was and shone her flashlight to find out. Loud cries of 'Sex maniac!', and worse, followed. Finally the usherette found a pair of scissors and freed the ponytail from the zipper. As his friend told Stanley afterwards, he never did get to see the main feature.

The *President Roosevelt* was the first American cruise ship to visit Taiwan for many years and there was a white uniformed band waiting to greet them on the wharf. As the ship came alongside the band solemnly played 'Land Of Hope And Glory' much to the bewilderment of the Americans on board the ship. There followed a dream two days to Hong Kong with the South China Sea a milky-white calm and covered with a heat haze. Junks would suddenly appear for a few seconds then disappear again like skimming dragon-flies.

We stayed at the old Repulse Bay Hotel with its magnificent openverandah dining room overlooking the South China Sea. Then we found an apartment in a block high above Deep Water Bay. With the apartment came a cookboy and an amah—Ah Lee and Ah Yee. Ah Lee translated as Mr Yee and Ah Yee as Number Two. But Chinese women have always got Women's Lib right. The Chinese family is a matriarchy. They were not only superb servants they took a great pride in their efficiency. The ultimate insult was if you tried to invade their domain.

One time when Joy and Morris West were visiting Hong Kong, the four of us came back to the apartment after a dinner party for a drink. It was late, around one in the morning. I snuck out into the kitchen to get some ice cubes and ten seconds later an indignant Ah Lee appeared, struggling into his white house coat and literally bundled me out of the kitchen. Two minutes later he was serving the drinks with his usual aplomb.

In any adoption there was a six-months' period when the child would live with you and a social worker would visit from time to time to make sure things were going well. A perfectly proper provision. One of the snags with a private adoption, our lawyer discovered, was that there was an aunt or uncle who would inevitably appear and demand money. If you didn't pay, they would threaten to claim the child. When the adoption was finally made legal, you had to make a statutory declaration that you had not paid any money to any of the child's relatives.

The thought of living for six months and not knowing from day to day when an aunt or uncle might suddenly appear on your doorstep was not to be contemplated. So what did we do now? Go back to the King of the orphans and tell him you're now living in Hong Kong, our lawyer said. We did, and the king of orphans said what a shame, this now places you in the lowest category of adopting parents. He then passed us on to his assistant.

The Prince of the Orphans would see us, always flanked by two Chinese social workers. He would then be rude and as provocative as he could, obviously hoping we would lose our tempers and he could then point out to the social workers how unsuitable we were.

We visited St Christopher's Orphanage and saw Andrew again. Then came a day when the Reverend Mr Osborne discovered that somehow Andrew had missed the net when all orphans had been made wards of the State and therefore he was immediately eligible for adoption. We made another appointment with the Prince of the Orphans and told him this. The Reverend Mr Osborne had primed us with the facts and figures, which Denise happily quoted chapter and verse.

'I will check', said one of the Chinese social workers quickly and disappeared before the Prince had a chance to open his big mouth. Back she came with a beaming smile on her face. It was absolutely correct. Andrew had been offered for adoption in America but, presumably because of his dropped foot, there had been no takers.

As we left the orphanage with Andrew, a number of the older boys were working in the gardens. They stopped working to watch us as we walked past them back to the car. All of them were in the twelve to fifteen age group and knew they were now too old to ever be adopted. The looks on their faces as they watched was something we would never forget.

For all the obvious reasons the diet at the orphanage was adequate but nothing more. At his first breakfast in the apartment Andrew asked for a boiled egg. The next morning he asked for two. By the time he got to five, Ah Lee was outraged, but we told him to serve them. Andrew managed four before he was ill. But he'd obviously proved a point to his own satisfaction. There was certainly enough food to go around.

There was an excellent Army school in Hong Kong which also took a few civilian's children to make up their numbers. We were lucky enough to get Christopher into there. Thereafter any correspondence from the school would always start: 'Your child, as a non-entitled child ...' It was enough to give anybody an inferiority complex.

There were twenty-four apartments in the block and most of them were occupied by either English or American families. All their kids had been primed about Andrew, the new arrival, and they should be nice to him. At the orphanage one of the prime ambitions of all the four-year-olds had been to become the Number One Fighter. Andrew was no exception. It made it hard to try and explain to various parents why, when their kids had been so nice to Andrew, lending him their toys and such, he repaid their kindness by beating the hell out of them.

Living in Hong Kong, with the help of Ah Lee and Ah Yee, became a sybaritic existence. There were a couple of snags. If you wanted to take a walk from where we lived you would have to drive the car to somewhere it was possible to take a walk. And the high humidity was always with you except for about six weeks in the year when it got so savagely cold you thought you really would have to wear a jacket when you went out. A lot of our friends visited Hong Kong when we were living there. We had a one-day routine. We would drive them out into the New Territories, have lunch at the floating restaurant at Shatin, go up to the border where they could actually see Red China— that was about as far as anybody got in the mid-1960s—then arrive at the Castle Peak Hotel with its fabulous view of the harbour, and have an ice-cold beer before coming back to Hong Kong Island itself.

For the visiting fireman who was there perhaps for just three days, it not only gave them a pleasant day out, it also enabled them to see a hell of a lot. We were always surprised at the number of people who would decline because they had to do their shopping, or have a new suit fitting, or something equally viable.

Rod Serling—the creator of the famous 'Twilight Zone' television series—and his wife visited, introduced by a mutual friend in Sydney. We invited them to dinner one night. He said friends of his, the Kramers, would also like to meet us. Bring them along, we said. Sidney and Esther Kramer were deeply embarrassed when they arrived because they thought it was to be dinner in a restaurant and they had invaded our privacy. We told them not to worry and it was a highly enjoyable evening. Sidney was then the President of Bantam Books. Later they took us to dinner in a very elegant hotel on the Kowloon side. As we were finishing dinner, Victor Weybright's name came up.

'And there he is now', Sidney said.

Sure enough, Victor Weybright was sitting at a table on the other side of the room. Sidney and I went over to say hello. Victor greeted me warmly. His first words were, 'What the hell are you doing with the opposition?'

Six months later Sidney Kramer was the President of NAL.

We made some good friends in Hong Kong. Paul Dunworth, our dentist, who did a masterly job of saving Jeremy's teeth, and his wife, Kaley. Jeremy's front teeth had been discoloured since the time he had had measles. Wait until he's around sixteen, our Sydney dentist had said, then I'll fix them.

'He won't have any front teeth by the time he's sixteen', Paul said. Then in the remaining two weeks before Jeremy had to go back to Sydney to school, he not only capped his four front teeth, but also rearranged his whole bite which had been the problem in the first place.

George Patterson, a writer and journalist who had covered the Chinese invasion of Tibet, had some fascinating stories to tell. We first met at a dinner party and I was seated next to his wife. A very charming woman but somewhat reserved, I thought; perhaps forced to live a little in the shadow of her husband's exciting career. I learned later she was a doctor and while George had been busy in Tibet she had been working in an Indian hospital under very primitive conditions, and the Indians gave her their highest award in gratitude when she left.

H'mmm. Just another example of a writer's infallible instinct.

The vast majority of the Hong Kong Chinese population were Cantonese. Hard-working, always cheerful, and with a very strong sense of humour. When we first adopted Andrew, Denise and I took lessons in Cantonese. Out of the two of us, she was the Number One Student and I was the Number Ten Student. I'm not sure now but I think there are eight different singing tones in Cantonese. The same word can have a completely different meaning, depending on how you say it, or 'sing' it.

Now, Tony Dawson-Groves was our doctor. His father had been a missionary in China and Tony had been brought up there until he later went to school in England. He spoke Mandarin, Cantonese, and about three dialects fluently. Diana, his Australian wife, was learning Cantonese and rang her dressmaker to make an appointment. In the middle of the conversation she suddenly realised both Tony and the houseboy were killing themselves with laughter.

'What was so funny?', she asked them. 'I only asked her what time would be convenient.'

'No, you didn't', Tony said, 'you asked her would she like an enema'. One of the stories I remembered from the Shanghai embassy just after the end of the war was about a whiz-kid who had done a twelve-month crash course in Chinese before arriving on the staff. At breakfast on his first morning in the embassy he was obviously determined to impress the rest of them at the table, so he launched into what sounded a tirade of Chinese. His basic problem was he had been taught Mandarin, the classic language of China, while the cookboy spoke Shanghai dialect. It went on for about five minutes until the cookboy suddenly beamed with comprehension.

'Ah', he said happily. 'You want egga!'

There was one time when I wanted to send a new manuscript urgently to New York. In the main post office I told the clerk I wanted to send it airmail express.

'I am sorry, sir', he said politely. 'We do not have any express mail from Hong Kong. But if you remove the cellotape from your package, I will provide you with some string to tie around it and you will save a considerable amount of postage.'

I gratefully did as he suggested then returned the package to him. He carefully stuck the stamps on, then equally carefully began to stick *Express* labels all over the package.

'I thought you told me there was no express mail from Hong Kong?', I said.

'That is perfectly true, sir', he said. 'But I do not think they know that in New York.'

In 1960 I had written a book called *Hong Kong Caper*. The Hong Kong background was based on my 1946 memories and it had been a very wild story about smuggling into Red China and so on. It was the sort of book I preferred to forget while I was living in Hong Kong, if you see what I mean.

One night George Patterson mentioned it, and I got that nasty sinking feeling in the pit of my stomach.

'I was just curious', George said, completely serious. 'Did you get any tip-off on that smuggling at the time?'

All out of my imagination, I confessed, and I had been waiting for him to fall about laughing.

'It was mild compared to some of the things still going on', George assured me. 'I can introduce you to a character tomorrow who'll fly anybody out of Red China if the price is right, for example.'

There came the day when Andrew was legally our child and we started to think about returning to Australia. He was put onto my passport, which was British, and at least the adoption problems we had had were over. Two days before we left a reporter from the then new afternoon paper, *The Star*, rang and said could she do an interview? That was fine, and the photographer took pictures of Andrew. The day before we were leaving, I had Andrew with me as I tried to finish off the final chores. Andrew decided he didn't want to walk. I knew he could walk, wasn't tired, and was just being bloody-minded. There was a lot to do and my temper was fraying fast. When he started to sit down on the pavement for the tenth time, I gave him a gentle boot in the tail to discourage him. Passers-by looked as if they were about to form a lynch mob so I hurried on. The next thing I saw was a newspaper placard which said 'Author adopts Chinese boy'. Now there's a coincidence, I thought. Wait a minute! I bought a copy of the paper and found we were on the front page. I wished I had the time to buy a couple more copies and mail them to the King and Prince of the Orphans.

We came back to Sydney in the *Iberia* and it was a great ten days with a placid sea the whole time. Another banana skin was waiting for me in the shape of a young customs officer who was feeling very important under his peaked cap. He was pinch-hitting for Immigration, I presumed. Denise and Christopher on their Australian passport went one way, me and Andrew on my British passport the other.

'Who is he?', the Peaked-cap demanded.

'My son', I said.

'I don't care about that', he said. 'He's Chinese.'

'The adoption was approved before we left Australia', I told him, then remembered the vital documents were packed in one of the crates in the ship's hold.

'He can't land', the Peaked-cap said firmly.

I finally suggested he get his office to ring Canberra and gave him the name of the senior official there and the approximate, but close, dates of the correspondence on file. He grudgingly said he would find out and we should wait in the cabin. He arrived back about an hour later and said we were being allowed ashore without prejudice but he wouldn't stamp my passport. Is that what Canberra said?, I asked wonderingly. Nobody in the Sydney office had been game to ring that high an official in Canberra, he said.

The Lord of the Banana Skins must have decided this was my day. To go ashore we had to pass through customs. A young customs officer asked me to open my briefcase. It contained three Australian Carter Browns. He examined them carefully, then shook his head slowly and said he didn't think he could allow me to bring them into the country.

'They were published here', I said, from between clenched teeth.

I opened one of them and showed him the Horwitz imprint; Sydney, Melbourne, Adelaide, etcetera.

'Okay.' He gave me a knowing wink. 'I'll let you bring them in.'

Three days later we went to Canberra. The British High Commission gave Andrew his own passport. The Australian

Government gave him the automatic right to unlimited entry into the country until he was eighteen, and then he could decide for himself which nationality he preferred. Some weeks later I had a phone call from the Sydney Immigration Office. If I liked to take my passport in they would stamp it for me, they said generously. If they wanted to send a man with a rubber stamp out to St Ives, I would let him stamp it, I said with equal generosity. Needless to say they didn't but I thought if I had never officially entered the country there was no way in which they could stop me leaving it the next time.

We settled back into a routine life at St Ives. Christopher and Andrew started at the St Ives Grammar School Prep; Jeremy was now at the main school. Priscilla had decided university life was not for her and achieved an advertising cadetship with one of the main departmental stores, Farmer's, now Myer. I was always an unasked-for big help. At one stage she was looking for a headline for a bra advertisement and I suggested, 'Girls, get your knockers up'.

These were the days when girls modelling underwear or bikinis still had their navels carefully airbrushed out. I don't know who it was who decided that the mere sight of a female navel would drive most of the male population berserk with lust, or why. I mean, what can you do with a navel?

*It wasn't so much the heat, more like the humidity. But Hong Kong's like that. I stood out on the balcony looking down at Deepwater Bay. A couple of water-skiers were swooping around but they didn't interest me. What did interest me was the pleasure Junk parked in the bay. I knew she had an armoury on board, and a couple of special engines fitted. Maybe later on we were going to need all the speed we could get out of her. I scraped a match down the side of the cookboy's face and put it to a cigarette. A couple of seconds later the doorbell rang. I let the cookboy answer it. He didn't like me answering it—I knew that because the last time I tried it he broke my arm. I checked out my strap watch and it said twelve noon; that meant George was right on time like always, except for the times he was late.*

*When he walked out onto the balcony I could see the tension in his face.*

*'All systems are go', he said. 'We leave at midnight.'*

*'Okay.' I shrugged gently. 'I'm ready.'*

*'How's your Mandarin?', he asked.*

*'You know I never eat oranges', I said.*

*Then, just to let him know I was kidding I sang him 'We'll Meet Again' in Cantonese.*

*'It's the Whang-Po Bay', George said, and wiped the sweat from his forehead with a Tibetan handkerchief. 'We wait for two hours and if they don't make contact we get the hell out of there.'*

*'What do we do while we're waiting?'*

*'Pretend we're fishermen.'*

*'We're not the right colour for it', I reminded him.*

*George's face tightened. 'I didn't spend all those years writing for the* London Observer *without some of it rubbing off', he said tightly. 'Just keep your racist ideas to yourself, all right? Some of my best friends are fishermen.'*

*'How about your old buddy with the airplane?', I said. 'Why can't he get them out?'*

*'The timing's all wrong for him', George explained. 'He's got a suit fitting the day after tomorrow and he's still got a hell of a lot of shopping to do afterwards.'*

*There was no answer to that. The idea of the caper didn't scare me. Nothing scares me after that Russian border incident. If I could handle those border guards with the tommy-guns the way I handled them at the time, I was ready to take on the whole goddamned Chinese Navy. More or less.*

*'You checked out the armoury?' I asked.*

*'Six bazookas, eight M1 rifles, six dozen grenades, and a four-inch howitzer', George said, 'and plenty of ammunition'.*

*I guessed it sounded adequate.*

'Who is the "them" we're picking up?', I prodded him.

'It's top secret.' George shrugged gently. *Maybe it was the sweat running down between his shoulder blades?* 'But as you're coming along with me I suppose you have the right to know. But you have no need to know. It's what they call a dichotomy.'

'Only one way to front up to a dichotomy', I said. 'Maintain an attitude of pragmatic ambivalence.'

George looked at me curiously. 'You never wrote for the Sydney Morning Herald at any time?'

'They were going to serialise one of my books a while back', I said. 'But at the last moment they substituted an article on sheep shearing for some reason.'

'It's not "them", it's a him.'

'It must be a real important him if we're going into the Whang-Po Bay to pick him up?'

George nodded. 'He's important all right. A top American publisher, as it so happens. He's been researching life in Communist China and he's going to write a book about it when he gets back. If we get him back that is. The problem is the Chinese saw the title of his book and that's why he's in deep trouble.'

'Just through the title of the book?'

'He called it The Ultimate Victor', George shook his head sadly. 'They figured he meant the United States of America.'

'Tough', I said sympathetically.

'You can say that again.'

'Tough', I repeated obligingly.

Suddenly George's whole body stiffened. 'What the hell?', he said incredulously, then his whole body slumped. 'Don't worry. I think we'll have to forget the whole thing.'

'What are you talking about?'

'Look!', he pointed dramatically towards Deepwater Bay.

I looked and suddenly realised the pleasure junk had completely disappeared.

'What the hell happened?', I asked, in a shaky voice.

'It's been sunk', George said despairingly. 'One of those bloody skimming dragon-flies again!'

We just stood there in silence for a couple of minutes, mourning the ultimate loser now forever marooned in the Whang-Po Bay.

'Hey!', George turned towards me with a faint look of hope on his face. 'You can't fly an airplane by any chance, can you?'

'I wouldn't mind trying, George', I said hastily, 'but I've got all these suit fittings coming up the day after tomorrow'.

# CHAPTER TEN
## THE TEN-DAY TRAIN

The Intimate Theatre progressed from strength to strength with Charles Walmsley producing most of the plays and David Goddard the balance. A children's group was also formed and Priscilla did some of their productions. There was a crisis Saturday when Jeremy had the four caps knocked from his front teeth while playing rugby in the morning and was due to appear as "the fairy swineherd" in Priscilla's production the same evening. Fortunately, not only had Paul Dunworth given him a spare set of caps originally, but also happened to be in Sydney at the time, and came to the rescue in the afternoon.

We had known Betty Archdale, the then headmistress of Abbotsleigh School, and her actor brother, Alexander, back in our Collaroy days when they used to visit friends who lived next door to us. Alex wanted to establish a professional theatre on the upper North Shore and Denise was interested in helping him. The Intimate Theatre unfortunately came to an end when the hall was pulled down. Among the stalwarts had been John Saunders, who is now the administrator of the Royal Academy of Dance in London; John Paramor, now a well-known and accomplished actor, John Townend, who later attended the London Film School and is now an entrepreneur, and Brian Eaton, who went on to the '680' Club. And all of them happily are still very good friends of ours.

Charles Walmsley also did some productions for the musical society in Goulburn. He once asked me to be the guest of honour at the opening night and I was naturally delighted. My speech at the end, after the final curtain, went something like: 'Blah, blah blah ... first class production ... blah, blah, blah ...

excellent performances ... blah, blah, blah ...'

There was a polite ripple of applause at the end of it then the audience made a concerted rush for the doors.

Later, Charles asked Denise to be the guest of honour. At dinner, before the show, Denise asked Charles if there was anything special he thought she should mention in her speech.

'Oh, yes', Charles said. 'Ray's worked like hell on the lighting, and Joan only came in to the production at the last moment because somebody fell sick and she's done a terrific job. Then there's—'

Denise mentioned every one of them in her speech. At the end, the cast behind her applauded wildly, the audience came onto its feet and applauded even more wildly. Nobody even started moving towards the doors.

H'mmm.

I wrote a book called *The Temple Dogs Guard My Fate* which was loosely a spy story based in Hong Kong. NAL published it in America and Canada. I wrote it under the pseudonym of Dennis Sinclair, a subtle variation of Denise Sinclair. It was also published in Germany and Italy, but didn't set anything on fire.

CB books had been published in Japan since early 1960 and I was intrigued when I got a copy of the first one. As opposed to the inevitable half-naked girl on the cover, the Japanese publisher had used a completely abstract painting. Betty Benjamin, the stalwart Rights and Permissions Manager of Horwitz, kindly wrote a letter for me to the Japanese publisher asking if I could buy the original painting. She received a courteous letter back which said unfortunately the original painting was not for sale. But, for the sum of £20 sterling, the artist would be happy to paint me another original of the original painting. I thought it showed up the lack of originality in Australian thought. Just take one small mental step forward and you can achieve a boundless number of originals from the one original painting. I offer this thought to all Australian artists freely.

What is now the Marion Street Theatre in Killara came into

being. Denise was on the board of directors and devoted a lot of time and energy to it. Priscilla was working at an advertising agency, W. B. Lawrence, and became in time a director of the agency. The boys' schooling progressed. Summer Saturdays became manic. Jeremy had taken up rowing and had to be at the boatshed by eight in the morning. The two smaller boys would be playing cricket, but for different teams, and would have to be taken off in different directions.

My parents visited us in Sydney in 1967. There was a cottage for rent at the time just across the road from us so they stayed there with Grace. They had planned on returning to England in November but Priscilla became engaged and the wedding was planned for early January, so they stayed on. A marquee was erected in the garden ready for the reception two days before and that was when the rain started and didn't stop until the morning of the wedding. As the wedding was taking place on a Saturday Priscilla had suggested the band hired for the occasion could play for the first dance either 'Where Are The Gentle Joys Of Maidenhood?' or, 'Never On A Sunday'. Unfortunately neither song was in their repertoire.

Father and daughter set off for the church in the back seat of a limousine, Priscilla clutching my arm tightly.

'I don't know', she said. 'I'm not sure about this at all. If I'm doing the right thing, I mean.'

'Don't worry, young lady', the driver said, in an unctuous voice. 'I've driven many brides-to-be to the church and, believe me, nearly all of them feel the same way as you do. But once you get into the church and the wedding ceremony starts you'll feel differently.'

'If you ask me', Priscilla said, 'it's all a fucking myth!'

The limousine careened sharply towards the curb, the driver just managing to correct the steering in time, then we spent the rest of the journey gazing at the back of his red and rigid neck. Priscilla was right. The marriage only lasted three months.

My parents went back to England and the life suburban

continued. We played a lot of weekend tennis with friends: Athlie and Alan Jacobs, Roma and John McMinn, Joy and Colin Mitchinson. We always played doubles and I was never a very good player. But at the end of the day one could happily remember the ace service and the low forehand that had just skimmed the net and kicked up the chalk inside the baseline. One never remembered the dreadful shots or the times one had missed the ball altogether. One was not stupid about games.

Holidays in Surfers Paradise I always thoroughly enjoyed. Part of the pleasure was the long drive to get there. Driving a car is one of life's great pleasures especially if you are slightly paranoid the way I am. The moment the car starts rolling, I start to feel relaxed. They can't get me now. They can't knock on the door, deliver a letter, or ring me up on the phone. *There is no way they can get me now!* That purring sound you hear as the car turns the first corner is me.

On the way up and back to Surfers Paradise we used to stay the night at an excellent motel just before Armidale. I used to enjoy it but the country always makes me feel nervous. Probably because I was born and bred on city pavements, and never mind what my mother says. The moment you switch the lights out in the country it is dark. *Dark.* Like you can't see your hand in front of your face. They don't even have street lamps. What they do have is a lot of beasties that go bump, or screech, in the night. Even worse, there are things that just make furtive rustling sounds. I'm not even happy driving at night in the country because I know they are rolling up the road behind me as I go along.

Australia's *grande dame* of theatre, Doris Fitton, asked Denise if she would manage the Independent Theatre for her. The Independent has a unique place in the history of Australian theatre. Founded by Doris and directed by her, it ran for forty-seven years and Doris was still there at the end. Robert Levis was the co-director when Denise joined the theatre and became a close friend through the years. Denise worked hard at the Independent and I had a lot of vicarious enjoyment from seeing shows I would otherwise not have seen, and taking part in the various Sunday night activities.

Jeremy left school and started at the New England University at Armidale. The two younger boys moved into the main school. By this time Andrew had had three operations on his dropped foot and it was now up to around eighty per cent normal usage. After the first operation when he was wearing a caliper for some months, he found it a very effective weapon indeed.

Then I heard that my father was ill. Both Denise and myself were only children and it sometimes has disadvantages. We decided to go to England and take the three boys with us. Priscilla, reasonably, preferred to stay in Australia where her career with the advertising agency was going well and she was enjoying it.

I could take one advantage from the move and that was fulfil a childhood ambition by travelling on the Trans-Siberian Railway. We flew to Hong Kong, stayed about a week while the bookings were confirmed, and enjoyed catching up with our friends. We took Ah Lee and Ah Yee to dinner at one of the floating restaurants in Aberdeen. With Ah Lee doing the ordering, we had a better meal than we could have ever achieved for ourselves and at about half the price.

The following night at a dinner party given by the Dawson-Groveses I sat next to a quiet American.

'How's the junk coming along?', somebody asked him.

He had been a successful businessman who, at the age of fifty, had decided he had done nothing of any great interest in his life and that did include making a lot of money. So he sold out to his partners and came to Hong Kong. He was having a large pleasure junk built to his own specifications which included air-conditioning. There was also a small armoury of guns and grenades lodged with the Hong Kong police, who would release them to him when he sailed. Piracy was still rife around the Philippines he had been told and you only warned off an approaching boat the one time. Then, if it kept on coming to-wards you, you lobbed a grenade into it.

'Where are you heading for when you leave here?', some-body else asked.

'New Zealand', he said. 'But I figure on taking a couple of years to get there.'

'And what will you do after you reach New Zealand?'

'I don't want to even think about that', he said seriously.

We sailed in the *Baikal*, a Russian ship that voyaged regularly between Nadhodka, Yokohama, and Hong Kong. It wasn't that big a ship—it looked like something Onassis might have kept on standby—but it was reasonably comfortable. When we left Hong Kong in the late afternoon the sea was absolutely flat and there wasn't a breath of wind. The boys even played table ten-nis on the upper deck. We established in the bar that the only reasonably-priced drink was Russian brandy, and you drank it with the best ginger beer I have ever tasted as a chaser. The food was a peculiar mixture of eastern and western styles that reduced your taste buds to a kind of nervous mumbling.

The weather started to get bad the following day and the day after that the typhoon struck with full force and stayed right with us until we finally reached Yokohama.

Most of the Japanese on board had taken the cruise down to Hong Kong and back again for their annual holidays. Appar-ently they had been hounded by another typhoon all the way down to Hong Kong. After exactly one day in Hong Kong they now had to endure another typhoon-hounded voyage back to Yokohama. Many of them preferred to stay on deck rather than face their cabins and they looked both ill and exhausted. You couldn't help imagining how it would be in casual conversation after they got home.

'Why, Fuji, you've lost weight since you went on your holiday.'

'Just over a stone, actually.'

'Did you diet?'

'No. All it needed was two weeks of vomiting and constant terror.' I wasn't sick but I came very close to it a couple of times and retired to my bunk. One night I woke up in the early hours of the morning and saw Denise standing in the cabin wearing a life-jacket.

'Why are you wearing a life-jacket?', I asked her.

'Because there's only one!', she snapped.

Most of the time the Captain had the ship on automatic pilot even through the typhoon. We were supposed to arrive in Yokohama at four in the afternoon. With this typhoon and this Captain we'll be lucky!, I sneered to myself. The ship came alongside the wharf in Yokohama at precisely 3.55 pm. It was only then I remembered the ship would make around twenty return voyages a year and the chances were the Captain had been doing them for at least the last five years.

We spent the night ashore in a hotel, luxuriating in the way it never even twitched when you walked across one of its floors. Our room had one window with a wooden shutter carefully drawn across it. Just one look at it and my claustrophobia sank its teeth straight into the back of my neck. Straight air-conditioned hotels are bad enough, the way they completely isolate you from the outside world and the real air. I quickly pulled back the wooden shutter so at least I could see the outside world still existed. Around five the next morning I woke up, opened my eyes, then screamed. The sun was shining through the window straight into my eyes.

We went back to the *Baikal*, back to sea, and back to that bloody typhoon which had veered out to sea but changed its mind when it saw we had sailed again and came back to keep us company to Nadhodka. The customs men went through our luggage carefully after we arrived. One of them went through a copy of a *Playboy* magazine Jeremy had with him very carefully indeed. We made the fifteen-hour rail journey to Khabarovsk where we joined the Trans-Siberian Railway to take us to Moscow.

Each coach had ten compartments and each compartment held four people. The top bunks folded down during the day to become the backs of the seats. Denise, myself, and the two younger boys were in one compartment. The Russians don't worry about mixing the sexes when they make up the numbers for each compartment, but Jeremy's hopes were dashed when he found himself sharing the next door compartment with three other young men. The journey would take nine days and the train would make eighty-four official stops. There was an eight-hour time change during the journey but you didn't have to worry about that because the train and all the station clocks kept Moscow time. It got to be confusing. It so happened one morning we had a pre-lunch drink then walked into the dining car to discover we were having breakfast.

At each end of the train was a bathroom with a washbasin and toilet. Our bedding was given to us after we boarded the train and was to last us until we reached Moscow. For the first two days it was a steam train, then diesel for the next two, and electric for the rest of the way. It was Summer and even Siberia could be hot and humid, so you had to open a window in the compartment. The coal smuts gently floated into the compartment during the first two days, blackening your bedding, your hair, and your clothes.

The menu in the dining car was written in Russian, German, and Japanese. One of the nicest things to have was fried eggs. They would bring them to you in a sizzling metal dish, still cooking. So then you could toss pieces of ham and cheese into the dish so it became a do-it-yourself omelette. We asked for a bottle of wine one night and the hardworking lady who ran the dining car brought us bottles of vodka and brandy in answer to our drinking mime, but finally produced a bottle of wine. To point up the triumph she lifted an empty wine-glass in a toast to us. 'Good evenink!', she said happily. We knew how to order wine after that with no trouble.

On our first visit to Moscow we had gone to the ballet and

returned to our seats after the interval, which meant a middle-aged lady and her aged mother had to get to their feet to allow us to pass. We thanked them in English, obviously, and suddenly a beatific smile illuminated the middle-aged lady's face.

'Dun—menshun—shit', she said proudly.

A Russian Army Major, his wife and two boys occupied the compartment on the other side of us. One early evening as the train was still passing Lake Baikal, the Major and I had a conversation. It must have lasted over an hour and it was all in sign language. We learned quite a lot about each other but it was exhausting. For the rest of the trip we smiled at each other in the corridor but kept on walking. Once was enough.

Siberia in Summer was beautiful and also experiencing the worst floods for thirty years which slowed the train down and sometimes brought it to unexpected halts, when half the passengers would get off and pick wildflowers. In our carriage were quite a number of different nationalities. A Japanese girl played her mandolin and some nights there was dancing up and down the corridor. When the train made its official stop at any station it lasted twenty minutes. There would be peasant ladies wearing kerchiefs selling local produce like bread, cheese, and milk. But nine days is still a hell of a long time to spend in a train, especially when you, your clothes, and your bedding seem to be steadily getting blacker all the time. Because of the floods, the train was fifteen hours late and arrived in Moscow around one am. By the time we got to the hotel it was about an hour later. The first bath turned the water black, the second turned the water grey, and the third didn't change the colour of the water at all.

It was August and there were 100000 foreign tourists in Moscow and they were all staying at our hotel. The meal coupons for the train, of course, could not be used in the hotel. So the next morning we had to join the queue at the Intourist desk to get our tickets. With the right tickets we could get breakfast. We joined the queue at eight-thirty in the morning and sat down to breakfast at eleven-thirty.

At Khabarovsk the Intourist lady had told us we could send our luggage separately in the luggage van by making a small payment. It was a brilliant idea and we did it. What we learned in Moscow was that the luggage van hadn't been attached to our train, but a later train which was now later still because there had been a derailment ahead of it. There was no way we were going to leave Moscow without our luggage so that meant extending our stay in Moscow. After about four days an Intourist lady suggested we go to the station and see for ourselves. She carefully wrote everything out in Russian for the cabdriver who took us to a station resembling Grand Central in size, disappeared for five minutes then came back shaking his head. Thanks a lot!

The next day Denise said we should hire a car and guide to see Moscow. See Moscow? I almost choked. We did that six years ago. And who the hell wants to see Moscow under these conditions. The way things are going we'll probably be here for another six months. Do it, Denise said. The guide was a pleasant girl in her mid-twenties.

'First, I will show you—'

'There's just one thing', Denise said. 'Do you think we could go to the station first? You see, our luggage—'

We went to the station first then much further to the goods depot the cabdriver had never found. The Russians have never bothered to breed guard-dogs. Instead, they clone guard-ladies. They are all in their early sixties, have iron-grey hair, a sergeant-major's voice, and the build of an all-in wrestler. Our guide argued her way past three of these and finally found our luggage just being unloaded onto a platform. It was an emotional moment.

Having missed our original booking to England we now had to wait for another one. We were offered a train to Warsaw and there we could wait for a train to London. We declined on the

basis nobody could guarantee to live that long. The next day a
fresh Intourist lady had another suggestion. She could send us
to East Berlin and then we could get to West Berlin and there
were many trains from there.

'How do we get from East to West Berlin?', we asked.

'There is a bus, I think.' She smiled brightly. 'I believe it is
very difficult.'

Again we declined. In the interim it seemed like a good idea
to get our Polish and East German visas, so we asked for our
passports.

'Do not worry about the other visas', the lady said, when she
looked at them. 'Worry about renewing your Russian visas.'

But it was obviously the hotel's fault as they kept our passports, and the Russian visas were extended within a couple
of hours. We then got our other visas after winning a savage
screaming match against a grey-haired clone at the East German Consulate.

It was a forty-eight hours' journey from Moscow to London.
There was a dining car attached to the train for the first evening
and that was it. We had been warned about this and had some
tinned food with us. Funny things seemed to be happening at
the Polish border. The train seemed to disintegrate into separate carriages, then were hoisted into the air while new sets of
bogies were run underneath them to cope with the narrower
gauge. It was a dreary journey and we were glad when we got to
Ostend and left the train. The journey across the Channel was
fine and we finally arrived at my parents' house around ten in
the evening.

I had mixed feelings about the Trans-Siberian, but I was
glad I had done it. The smart thing we supposed would have
been to leave the train every second day and stay overnight in
a hotel where you could have a bath and change your clothes,
apart from any other delights that might be lurking around
the corner. It had certainly been different from the time Peter
Fleming had made the journey in 1936, I think. I had read his

account when I was a schoolboy. In those days the journey took two weeks and you bought your food, like live chickens, before you started, and also made your arrangements with one of the cooks on the train to take care of you during the journey.

My father's health began to improve slowly. Perhaps having given up smoking two years earlier at the age of seventy-three had a lot to do with it? We began to sort ourselves out, first finding a flat. Old friends, Simone and Roy Goulston, had helped organise a special entry exam at Dulwich College for the two younger boys. Later, when buying the school uniforms, I remembered I only had travellers' cheques with me. They were no problem in central London but I had found on a couple of other occasions outside London people had no idea what they were. Better to broach the subject earlier than later, so I asked the gentleman serving us at the school's commissariat if he would mind being paid in travellers' cheques? Of course not, he assured me. Then, with my inevitable compulsion to explain things in no need of explanation, I told him my reasons for asking.

'I quite understand, sir', he said. 'Only the other day a minor supplier—socks, or something equally trivial—asked me for a reference. Well! I said to him we've only been here for four hundred years. Will that do?'

I knew we were back in England.

February 4, 1981.

Mr Brown:

My name is ————. I'm in state prison at Soledad, California, doing twelve years eight months for four counts of attempted murder, that I did not do. I have an appeal in but I don't know when I will be going back to court. The reason I'm writing you is that I'm a writer and I've written a book about my life and it's

a good book. It's all about from day one, when I was
bom in a little town in the backwoods of Mississippi.
When I moved to Detroit from there to Minnesota,
from there to California where I got in this trouble.
I'm thirty-three years of age and never been in trouble
with the law until now. I don't have any money but if
you can help me publish this book I'm sure we can
work out something. It's a good book and I'm sure it
will sell big. If you are not interested please forward
my idea to someone you know.

Thank you, sir,

A troubled man.

# CHAPTER ELEVEN
## BUT WHAT I MEANT ...

The letter on the preceding page is genuine and I have the writer's permission to quote it. Obviously, I will help him in any way I can. I don't envy any writer starting today, except the ones that get a million dollars advance for their first book. There aren't too many of those, either. The short story market has almost completely disappeared and nobody is doing those wonderful 20000-word novelettes anymore.

I can remember the days when Victor Weybright of NAL would publish a book because he thought it should be published. The same would certainly have been true of Bennett Cerf of Random House, and Alfred Knopf. But I doubt if there is anyone still around today with the same literary clout as they had. Since the multinationals started diversifying in the late 1950s and 1960s, it's hard to find a publishing imprint which is not part of a group, which is not part of a division of an oil company or something similar (at least in multinational size). And the emphasis becomes increasingly on the 'big' book. If you pay a million dollars, or more, advance for a book, you are obviously determined to make a profit on it. Reviewers are going to be impressed and, even if they hate the book and say so, they will tend to give it prominent reviewing space. And so on. About a year back I was talking to an American who distributes paperbacks in New York State.

'I never thought I'd live to see the day they advertised books on television', he marvelled. 'I give it ten years at most before I'm out of business. By that time each publisher will be publishing one title a month, having paid a three million dollar advance for it.'

Could be. Certainly, the million-dollar advance leaves a lot less money available for risk on other books and other writers. So, I think I'm lucky to have started writing when I did. There must be a statute of limitations on how long you continue to write without selling anything. I think I was getting close to it when Invincible actually accepted my first Western.

I have been lucky with editors from Lyall Moore in his editorial days to Ed Doctorow. Whenever you receive any editorial criticism, you have to allow five minutes for the ego's fury to subside. How dare anybody criticise any part of your perfect work, you reasonably ask yourself. Then, when you've cooled off, you take another look and ask yourself if the editor is justified and find he almost invariably is. I used the word *he* in its collective meaning of *he*, *she* or *it*, thereby hopefully covering all indignant minority groups.

Titles are something else again. A book title cannot be copyrighted which is just as well for everybody concerned, especially me. Gather a number of mystery writers together then ask all those who haven't written books entitled *Murder Is My Mistress* and *Venus Unarmed* to put their hands up. You will notice that not many hands go up. Mine certainly doesn't. Cute titles are always the dangerous ones.

One time I called a book *The Dream Is Death*. It's vitally important a title has something to do with the content of the book and to that extent it was a good title. A long letter from my NAL editor at the time said they had just done some market research and found the word 'death' in a title was very unpopular so they would have to change the title. It made sense and I didn't argue. The book was published as *The Dream Is Deadly*.

In the time when folk music was making it in a very big way I called a book *The Ballad Of Loving Jenny*. I even wrote some lyrics to go with it and to be sung to the tune of 'Hanging Johnny'. Nobody could say CB wasn't right up to date and on the ball. It was published as *The White Bikini*.

One book had a very strong ballet background and I called

it *The Balletomaniacs*. You'll never guess. It was published as *Dance of Death*, and with no apologies to Augustus Strindberg, either.

If you'll excuse me for a moment, but just about here seems the right place for a quick note to my publisher Bill Reed:

*Bill, I think this book should be called* Ready When You Are, C.B.!, *if that's alright with you. A.Y.*

*Alan, it's all right by me. But I don't quite get the connection. B.R.*

*Bill, it's like this: Once Cecil B. deMille was shooting a Western and had taken his backers out on location with him. 'Gentlemen', he said expansively, 'you see the valley below you. In two minutes' time a thousand Indians will come charging in from the East. They will be met by a thousand US cavalrymen charging in from the West. From the South will come a rampant herd of buffalo—and the three elements will meet in a dreadful head-on confrontation that will last eight minutes on film, will cost five million dollars, and be worth every cent.'*

*So it all happened and the backers were very impressed indeed. When it was all over deMille turned to the cameraman beside him and asked how it was. The pale cameraman, his whole body shaking, said, 'I don't know how to tell you this, Mr deMille, but the camera jammed the moment the action started and I haven't got one foot of it'.*

*The backers looked nervous. deMille smiled and looked at the second cameraman and asked him how it was. The also-nervous cameraman said his camera had sprung a light leak and every foot of film was fogged and useless. By now the backers were very nervous indeed. deMille smiled at them. 'Gentlemen', he said fondly, 'you forget I am Cecil B. deMille. I never leave anything to chance. Right on top of that bluff over there is my top-rated cameraman, Ike. And he's there to cover any accidents like we've just had. Give me a walkie-talkie'. Somebody does and deMille speaks into it.*

*'How was it, Ike?'*

*'Ready when you are, C.B.', came the confident reply. A.Y.*

*Alan, I see what you're driving at and agree with the title. B.R.*

*So how come I don't get asked? A.W.*

One of the inevitable questions that makes a writer uneasy is: 'Where do you get your plots from?'

The answer should be: 'There's this great little store just behind the town hall'.

The true answer is the writer never knows. He knows what started him off—an idea of a theme, an intriguing character, an opening situation, but the rest has been a combination of hard work, despair, outrage, and patience (using The Devil's Dictionary, which defines patience as a minor form of despair disguised as a virtue.) There must be many writers who can sit at their desks and carefully plot out the whole book before they start. I have tried it a couple of times but it never works for me. One of the main projected characters is so boring the typewriter yawns every time I write his name, while that minor character who was supposed to have been killed on page eight is starting to sound like fun.

Would-be writers ask you for advice on how to write. The only answer on how to write is to write. Go away and do it. Don't tell me you have this brilliant story in mind. Every story in the mind is brilliant, and if you tell enough people about it your ego will have had enough false stimulus to make sure you will never actually do the hard part and write it. If you want to know what to write, ask a publisher. They can always tell you exactly what to write ... as close a replica as you can get, short of plagiarism, of the last big-seller on their list. Or anybody else's list, come to that, if it sold enough copies.

When I started out I read all the books on how to write I could find, and read the magazines avidly. Apart from basics—type your manuscript and double-space it and leave a decent margin on the lefthand side—they didn't seem to help me very much. The one excellent piece of advice was an article about the Come-to-realise story. We all know it. The story where the reader and everybody else concerned knows the answer but the main character hasn't yet come to realise he should use a deodorant or that Charlie already knows he's seduced his wife, or whatever the problem is. One of the great problems of the earlier science fiction movies was just that. The audience knew the Martians had landed from the first two minutes into the movie, but then they had to hang around and wait another hour until the cast began to figure out what had happened. The same boring approach has been used in quite a few detective television series, which open by showing you the murderer commit the murder and then you have to hang about for the next fifty minutes until the detective catches up.

In the late 1960s NEL reprinted a CB book *The Lover*. Fate took a hand and the printer who received the job had also printed a collection of short stories by Daphne du Maurier under the same title, about twelve years before.

'Of course', somebody said, 'we've still got the plates.'

So the book had a girl in a gold bikini on the cover, and the collection of Daphne du Maurier short stories as its contents. Gerry Morse, who was the Assistant Managing Director of NEL at the time said they recalled the books as soon as the mistake was discovered but had to write to Daphne du Maurier, tell her what had happened and confess they could not guarantee that no copies had been sold. Daphne du Maurier wrote back saying not to worry and she had long ago learned not to judge any book by its cover.

Maurice Dolbier, who edited the book page of the *New York Herald Tribune* at the time we were living in New York, was visiting one night and saw my electric typewriter.

'I've never used one of those', he said. 'Do you mind if I try it?' 'Help yourself', I told him.

So he sat down at the typewriter and wrote the best opening line to a novel I have ever seen before, or since. It has everything: intrigue, suspense, sex; you name it. Maurice's opening line was:

'My God!' he said. 'It's Lola. Whoever she is?'

# CHAPTER ONE
## TO BE CONTINUED ...

*She opened the front door wide then just stood looking at me. I looked right back at her because looking any place else would have been a real waste. Her glossy black hair was cut short so it fit the contours of her head like a helmet, and her black eyes said she knew it all and had possibly rewritten the book. She was wearing ... I don 't know what the hell to call it. It covered her from shoulders to ankles, was made out of some white material which was almost completely transparent. Her full breasts thrust against the flimsy fabric, the nipples making indentations, and I could see at the tops of her long curving legs a delicate black triangle was outlined.*

*'Who the hell are you?', she asked coldly.*

*'Lieutenant Wheeler, from the sheriff's office. ' I showed her my tin. 'I've come about the body.'*

*'Don't push your luck just because I happen to be wearing something revealing', she said.*

*'I've come about the other body', I said patiently. 'The dead one that belongs in the morgue.' I had a sudden dreadful suspicion. 'You are Lola?'*

*'I'm Lola', she agreed. 'What are you? Some kind of a nut?'*

*'If you're Lola, then you called in around a half-hour back and reported a homicide, right?'*

*She shook her head. 'Wrong.'*

*It looked like it was going to be one of those nights when ...*

(It's about time. Back to reality at last! A.W.)

This print edition published in collaboration with Brio Books,
an imprint of Booktopia Group Ltd

Level 6, 1A Homebush Bay Drive · Rhodes NSW 2138 · Australia

Print ISBN: 9781761280627

briobooks.com.au

| MIX | The paper in this book is FSC® certified. |
| --- | --- |
| Paper from responsible sources | FSC® promotes environmentally responsible, |
| FSC® C008194 | socially beneficial and economically viable |
| | management of the world's forests. |